Golden Tales
Havoc in Rome

By I.V. Everts

Illustrations by Marjan Rahimi

First Edition 2019

Printed in the United States of America

A 2 Z Press LLC

PO Box 582

Deleon Springs, FL 32130

bestlittleonlinebookstore.com

sizemore3630@aol.com

440-241-3126

ISBN: 978-1-946908-71-1

Dedication:

To Alberto for giving me

the freedom to do what I love.

GOLDEN TALES

INTRODUCTION

INTRODUCTION

My little book is about Texel, my Golden Retriever puppy, and me and the havoc we - mainly 'she' - cause in Rome. Texel is naughty. The problem with her is, besides being naughty, she is also very bright and beautiful. She uses these attributes to steal umbrella's, seeing glasses, hats, and most of all food - any food. Some find her as charming as I do, and some, not so much.

We live in Rome, Italy. In addition to my cute little dog's mishaps, I also included some fun facts about Italy because Rome is gorgeous and I felt these sights and attractions add interest to our little stories. We hope you agree.

Texel is actually an Island in the Netherlands, which is pronounced, 'Tessel.'

We hope you enjoy reading about our adventures as much as we enjoyed making our memories and writing about them.

Chapter 1

THE PARK

Welcome to Rome.

I want to take a few pages to share about some areas in Rome that Texel, my beautiful Golden Retriever, and I visit so you as my reader can see what we see and enjoy here in our Rome home. I included highlights in each chapter. One lovely area we visit frequently is called the Villa Borghese.

Villa Borghese is a garden park. It is a popular tourist attraction enjoyed by many tourists as well as every Italian in Rome - including Texel and me. This Villa is often called the largest open-air museum in the world because it is home to the

Borghese Gallery (above) which houses the historical and valuable paintings of famous artists like Leonardo da Vinci, Caravaggio, Tiziano (Titian) and more. This museum is very popular and an appointment to visit is necessary.

King Umberto I (the good King)

In addition to the Gallery, there are many sculptures, such as the one above of King Umberto, small fountains and a picturesque lake. The Villa is also home to about 100 turtles, 60 ducks and dozens of other water birds including swans and geese. It is very peaceful amidst the hustle and bustle of Rome.

One of my favorite attractions in the Villa Borghese is the L'Orologio ad acqua. This hydro chronometer - also known as a water clock - was built in 1867 by the inventor Giovan Battista Embriaco. He displayed this water clock at the Universal Exposition of 1867 in Paris. Please take my word for it, it is a fantastic structure, but the time is never right.

The lovely Villa Borghese is the third largest park in Rome and spans almost 200 acres. It is located on a hill called the Pincian Hill. (which does not happen to be one of the Seven Hills of Rome).

We have had many great adventures in the park.

I want to take a moment to talk about the Seven Hills in Rome because I refer to them again in later chapters. Today, five of the seven hills - the Aventine, Caelian, Esquiline, Quirinal, and Viminal Hills, are the sites of monuments, buildings, and parks. As for the other 2 - the Capitoline Hill is the location of Rome's city hall, and the Palatine Hill is part of the main area in Rome dedicated to the scientific study of historic and prehistoric peoples and their cultures by analysing their artefacts, inscriptions, monuments, and other such remains; especially those that have been excavated. There is much culture and history everywhere you look in Rome.

These beautiful stairs are one entrance into the park to the area of the Pincio terrace. Since the park is situated on a hill, it makes for quite a spectacular view of many areas of Rome. This terrace in the Pincio is in the southern area of the Pincian Hill and provides just that spectacular view of Rome.

Yes! As can be seen, the Pincian terrace offers a panoramic view over Rome that is breath-taking. Some sights in Rome should never be missed. Most whirlwind trips to Rome always include the grand sites like the Colosseum, the Pantheon, Trevi Fountain and the Vatican, but it would be a mistake to skip the Pincio Terrace.

One majestic sight from the terrace is the view of the Basilica of St Peter in the Vatican. This is undoubtedly one of the most romantic panoramic views in Rome overlooking domes, roof tops, and other various buildings in this over two-thousand-year old city.

If you walk over to the left side of the Pincio terrace, you will see the wonderful 'Altare della Patria' in the distance.

The Altare della Patria is the altar of the homeland where the Unknown Soldier lays guarded 24/7, 365 days a year, by two members of the armed forces. If in luck, one may even see the changing of the guards.

Just a few of the lovely sites of the famous city.

As I am certain you can appreciate, there are so many wonderful areas of Rome that can be seen from the terrace.

The Pincio faces the west in the Villa Borghese Park, so, if you come at sundown you can enjoy seeing the city at this golden hour! The warm orange glow of the setting sun casts a soft, almost velvet appearance to the exterior structures as it reflects off the ancient architecture.

One of my very favorite areas in the Villa Borghese Park near the Pincio terrace is another entrance into the terrace area called the Piazza del Popolo.

This awesome view can be seen while standing on the terrace. I could stand here for hours enjoying the view.

View of the Piazza del Popolo from the Pincio terrace.

The Piazza del Popolo, known as the people's square, is located in the center of Rome and is just inside the northern gate of the city of Rome. One of the most famous sites here is an Egyptian obelisk dedicated to Ramesses II called the Flaminio Obelisk. It is a tall monument located in the center of the piazza. As can be seen in this photo, a spectator can also see the buildings around and beyond the square.

This picture is the amazing view of the Pincio terrace on the Pincian Hill looking up from Piazza del Popolo.

Another of my very favorite landmarks in Rome are the stunning Spanish steps.

I mention the steps in a later chapter, but wanted to include them here since they are also a way to enter the Villa

Borghese Park for a relaxing day of fun. It is just a short ten-minute stroll up the steps into the park.

After coming to the Villa Borghese and taking in this sweeping vista across Rome from the Pincio and seeing the Piazza del Popolo and the steps and more, visitors can take a quiet and relaxing stroll around the regal spaces of this beautiful park along many paths to view the two hundred twenty-eight busts of great nineteenth-century Italians and other Europeans. The occasional blemish or graffiti are quickly dismissed by onlookers as they admire the beauty of the aged structures. The Villa Borghese has pathways that are also lined with fountains already briefly mentioned and a church and the Silvano Toti Globe Theater is here as well.

With this brief introduction to Rome and the Villa Borghese Park, I am certain one can see why my husband, our Golden Retriever, Texel, and I call and love Rome as our home.

No matter how long I live here, I am overwhelmed with beauty each time I visit these areas of Rome.

Chapter 2

THE HANDBAG HEARTBREAK

Rome is certainly lovely. This chapter is about our first adventure together - our encounter of the most unpleasant kind to be honest.

On many and great days, Texel and I spend our time leisurely walking together amidst all the Roman splendor in the dog park of Villa Borghese that is called Valle dei Platani; which is next to a bio-park. The bio-park is a visitor attraction that combines a few aspects of a zoo with a botanical garden and has animals placed within to re-create their natural habitat. Texel has a great time running up and down the hills and rolling around in the grass in the Valle dei Platani !!!

As I mentioned in the first chapter, this park is in the center of the city but, being a large park, makes you feel as if you are in the countryside; apart from everything else in the world. What are a happy duo Tex and I are!!!

In the Valle dei Platani, dogs are permitted to run free. Many of the dogs enjoy the game of chasing the squirrels in the park. Here, Texel is able to run freely without being scolded and I enjoy the walk, the fresh air, and the lovely sounds of nature.

Some of my favorite sounds are the little green parrots that frequently escape from the Zoo, which runs alongside the dog park and have made their home in the Valle dei Platani. The peculiar sounds of the sea gulls, which arrive from the nearby river Tiber, can also be heard as we walk along.

The Tiber River (Tevere in Italian) is the third longest river in Italy - flowing 405 KM (252 miles) through areas like

Tuscany, Umbria, and Lazio. It has become famous as the main watercourse in Rome but has a current that is too dangerous to make swimming in it possible.

As we walk along, I hear the seagulls squawking, chirping and wailing as they respond to the distant caws of other seagulls. I especially love hearing the zookeepers 'wake-up' the tigers, donkeys and others. I almost feel as if I am back in Africa or near the Sea.

Each visit we soak in the vast splendor found here - more than we could have ever imagined - in our homeland in Rome. However, not all the people are as beautiful as the sites Texel and I see each day. To be truthful, Texel always expects everyone to love her as much as she loves everyone and, unfortunately, it just doesn't happen that way many times.

To understand how Texel and I got into our bit of trouble this day, one must understand Italian culture. Italians judge others by appearance. As the world knows, Italians are known for great Fashion and Style. Not only do they value beautiful clothing and style, families - mothers-in-laws included - judge others on the basis of physical beauty.

To be blunt, they judge people who are beautiful differently than people they consider 'not beautiful.' It comes as no surprise that the Italian phrase 'fare una bella figura' literally means 'make a beautiful person or figure.' It is used when someone does the 'correct' or proper thing at the 'correct' or proper time. Correctness and properness are considered 'beautiful' as well as physical beauty and financial endowment.

The standard used to judge people is not only if they are fashionably dressed, it applies to locations where they live, cars they drive, and even gyms they frequent. All these status identifiers let the world know one is doing well and is 'someone' in Italy. I can imagine it is the same in other places.

To be honest, to most in Italy, and, probably the entire world, Texel and I are just ordinary. We are not flashy or wealthy, but we are happy.

Today, our 'average' status got us into a bit of a troublesome situation. While walking with Texel in the park, I spotted a woman in the distance. At first, I thought she was in the park with a dog and waiting for it to return to her. However, as I came closer, all my own feelings about different people of different social status came over me.

As we walked toward the woman, I realized she was a typical, 'Pariolina' (a resident of Parioli). I have to say Parioli is a beautiful, but snobbish area in Rome. And, as a rule, the people from Parioli are also beautiful, but snobbish. I did what I thought was the polite thing to do and I set my feelings aside and made an effort to greet her. She ignored me.

For all the reasons that don't make sense to me, ladies from Parioli think they are deities. There are several different ways ladies from Parioli see people they do not know.

As they look at you, they seem to do a quick check and ask themselves, "Are you super wealthy or are you poor?" "Are you the granddaughter or daughter of a wealthy family?" "Are you famous? If so, you can become a great party attribute." "Do you hold a title such as Baroness, Earl, or Prince?" (These titles are absurd, by the way, because Italy became a republic in 1946 and is not a monarchy. Nevertheless, the Italians hang onto these classifications for dear life.) I could see her thinking.

My status is easy. It is essentially 'none of the above.' This being the case, I am considered a "persona non grata"! - Which means an unacceptable or unwelcome person and therefore I am not worth greeting - or maybe just granted a glance, but cold and aloof!!!

I have accepted my lot in life, but Texel, however, refuses to be ignored. She conforms to no social standard in Rome. She wants to show everyone, including this lady, her playfulness! She always wants to make friends no matter how wealthy someone may be because she just cannot see differing social classes. Bless her for that!

So, Texel did the unthinkable. As we neared, she pulled at my hand on her leash and lounged up at the lady. "OOPS!!! Big mistake!!!" I thought.

I tried to apologize and keep walking, but Texel did not want to merely walk by; she was determined to make friends. I cannot stop her.

Next, Texel began running around the lady like a dog herding sheep!!! Then, she committed another unthinkable and unforgivable act. She jumped up at the lady's handbag and had the absolute audacity to give it a lick with her long wet tongue!!! This must be a naughty dog's way of saying 'hello.'

With my mouth wide open, awaiting this hoity-toity lady's response, I saw her face turn to thunder!!! It was as red as any red I have ever seen. Her lips pursed with anger and at first she was speechless. Texel started running toward her again.

I knew we were in a bit of trouble, so I frantically tried to collect Texel, but it was almost impossible. I nearly broke my neck trying to run in my wellies (my rubber rain boots).

Attempting to avoid falling or tripping over tree roots, I waved my arms in a large circular motion for balance. To make matters worse, the area was wet from recent rain; making everything in our crime scene more treacherous.

During our struggle to get away from the woman, Texel and I heard her screaming!!! We managed to get some distance away and, since she was too far away for me to hear and I could only hear loud words, I shouted over my shoulder, "What is the problem?" as we began walking back in her direction.

When we were close enough to make out her words, I clearly heard her insulting me. Over and over, she kept calling me a foreigner without manners. "What is the problem?" I asked again.

She fumed, "Your dog licked my handbag!!!"

At that moment she reminded me of Victoria Beckham; petite and pretty. For those who do not know Victoria Beckham, she is an English businesswoman, fashion designer and former singer. In the late 1990s, Beckham rose to fame with the all-female pop group, Spice Girls, and was dubbed Posh Spice by the July 1996 issue of the British music magazine Top of the Pops.

Don't get me wrong, I like Victoria Beckham, but she is not famous for having a warm, smiling face. Some even think she is a snob. Hence, the resemblance.

I started laughing and was unable to stop myself as the many funny thoughts swirled through my mind, "Who gets angry when a puppy licks a handbag in a dog park. Oh please, let's call the fashion police!!!"

I then reminded her, "This is a dog park, signora!!!"

She shouted, "THIS BAG IS AN HERMES!!" (pronounced air-mez) as though she was holding the Holy Grail, but it really is just a designer handbag (a little bag worth a mere $12-300,000).

Well, I guess if I was not a poor girl and had a Hermes of my own, I would not want a young, lovable, playful, beautiful, naughty Golden Retriever to put her wet tongue on it either; but I am not rich and do not have a designer bag like that. Nevertheless, I do have a dog like that.

So many thoughts flooded my brain all at once. I wanted to scream insults back at her like, 'Your Hermes is so last season!' or 'Are you sure you didn't buy it on the black market, it looks fake?' I, however, decided to be nice and apologize - after I made the point *again* that she was in a dog park, not at a fashion show!!!

Sometimes things are sure frustrating.

Still, slightly shaking in my Wellingtons, I decided it was best to get as far away from this lady as possible. She, however, refused to accept my apology and continued shouting insults at me as Texel and I walked on.

I looked at Texel and said: "MA E' PROPRIO MATTA!" which means, SHE IS TRULY CRAZY. Texel just wagged her tail as we continued on. We try our best to stay out of trouble when we visit the Villa Borghese Park. It is not easy to do with a pup like Texel!

Chapter 3

TEXEL AND THE SEA

It was another beautiful day in Rome one early morning in April when we - my husband and I and Texel - decided to make the most of the excellent weather.

Just as the sun popped out, we all hopped in our car and drove to the seaside for a nice long walk on the beach. Our interest was not only a stroll along the sand; we wanted to introduce Texel to the sea and the beach.

My in-laws have a large beach house in Tor San Lorenzo - one we used to stay at often - but with the arrival of Texel, we are no longer invited; we are not even permitted in the garden! My in-laws are not dog people, or maybe they are just not 'Texel' people. Either way, we are banned. Sad, sad, sad for us.

At first, when we arrived that morning, we had the beach to ourselves. Miles and miles of coast line lie ahead of and behind us. My husband and I walked hand in hand as we enjoyed the roaring sounds of the waves crashing over and coming in and going out all morning.

My husband listens well as I carry conversation for both of us. This makes us a perfect match. I am the talker and he is the listener. For hours, the three of us walked along the sea on the beach talking, laughing, and leaving only footprints in the sand.

Texel ran freely alongside us. She darted in and out of the water splashing us as she came bounding back in our direction. All in all, everything was terrific and Texel was having a ball!!! She was a natural at the sea and in the sand; just like her owners.

As we walked, we talked about how we are not allowed in my in-law's house, and decide this is still our favorite beach.

Tor San Lorenzo is north of Anzio - which is better known for the Battle of Anzio that took place during WWII starting January 22, 1944 with the 'Allied amphibious landing' known as 'Operation Shingle' ending

on June 5, 1944 with the capture of Rome by American troops. This capture forced German troops to withdraw from the area.

While recalling our very important Roman history and, very suddenly, we were interrupted as a jogger, who seemed to come from nowhere, came our way!!!

Our lonely little section of the beach was suddenly and unexpectantly invaded by this man running rapidly toward us.

We instantly sensed trouble for Texel; who had been unleashed since we hit the sand. We were unable to find a way to distract her quickly.

Just then I noticed Texel noticing the jogger. With her nose pointed at him and her body lurching in his direction, I knew she was in her running mode!!! Before we could snap her leash, our little four-month old fluff was bounding her way down the beach to greet this jogger. I called over and over for her to come back, but, to no one's surprise, she ignored me completely!!!

My husband and I started running after her and found ourselves slipping in the sand as we dove trying to grab her. What a site we were! We were glad we did not see anyone there taking videos of us.

The jogger, a young man in his thirties, and quite a distance in front of us, started screaming desperately, '*Signori, get your dog!!!*'

We thought his reaction was a bit exaggerated because Texel was wagging her tail and she really was only a puppy. We couldn't understand how he did not realize she meant no harm. If he just reached down to pet her, we were certain the whole encounter would be over quickly. He didn't.

Nevertheless, we continued calling Texel while we slipped and fell on all fours in the mud and sand running to catch her. The only thing we managed to accomplish was filling our mouths with sand. Our little girl seemed to turn into a greyhound when she was on a mission to make a new friend!!!

We tried shouting to the jogger, "She is not dangerous. *She is only a puppy!!!*" He dismissed us altogether.

As Texel reached the petrified jogger, he began screaming louder, "*Signori*, get your *#^!* dog" and more Italian insults came our way!!!!

Then, to our surprise, the frantic jogger became so panicked, he dove into the freezing sea water!!! To be honest, we were stunned. Then, to make matters worse and, just when he thought he was safe, Texel jumped right in after him! Her mission was undeterred; after all, she is a water dog!!! Bet he didn't see that coming.

We were amazed and proud of her at her strong swimming ability as she swam with all her power to reach the man. She must have thought, '*This dude needs saving!!!*' and she was going to save him!

When he realized he could not evade the puppy, he swam back to shore; still petrified!!! - of a little, happy, golden puppy. Oh geez!

We caught up with both of them and finally had Texel's attention. As we clipped her leash, we breathed a sigh of relief. The wet, frozen, frightened, angry man ran away. He was dripping from head to toe as he ran along the beach to his home - to safety. To be honest, we were grateful the whole event was over.

Texel looked up at us with her innocent expression as if to say, "Yeah! Yoo-hoo, that was fun."

That may not be what the jogger was thinking.

We hoped the jogger did not fall sick with bronchitis. We were truly sorry he was so frightened.

Chapter 4

SWIM TIME FOR TEXEL

As I mentioned, there are so many beautiful sites in Rome. Some of the most spectacular sites include Rome's well known fountains and, believe me, they are spectacular!

In addition to the Villa Borghese, Texel and I visit them every chance we get. One of my very favorite fountains is the famous Trevi Fountain. It is also called the Fountain of Love.

Trevi is close to the Villa Borghese Park. In fact, if Texel and I walk through the Piazza del Popolo, we can casually stroll about 20 minutes along the streets of Rome - window shopping as we go. Texel is the best shopping buddy. She, like me, can shop all day.

One street we stroll down often, Via del Corso, is a very busy shopping street. Here we find all the commercial shops. Also located on Via del Corso 18 is the museum of the German poet Johann Wolfgang Goethe.

When we walk almost to the end of Via del Corso, we see a shopping Gallery on the left called 'Galeria Alberto Sordi.' It is very pretty and is a lovely place for a cold tea or ice coffee in the summer. Sometimes Texel and I stop in.

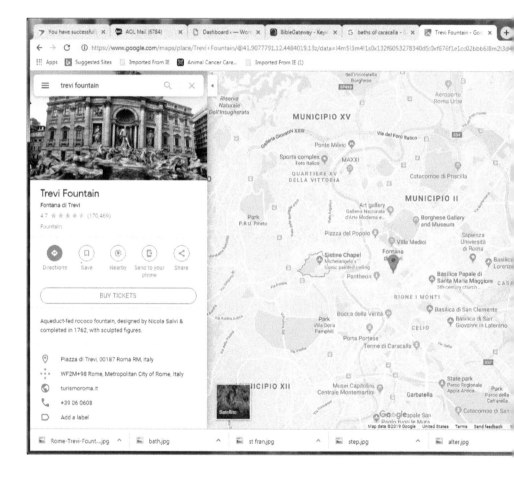

Just after the gallery, we turn left onto Via dei Crociferi. At the end of this road we find the lovely Trevi Fountain.

The Trevi Fountain is very well guarded, so if I would try to let Texel swim there, I would probably go to jail. Many others - including tourists - have tried.

Although the Trevi Fountain is only a 20-minute walk from the Pincio, most people take an entire day for this because of all the many shops in between.

Trevi is the most beautiful fountain in Rome. It is 20 meters (65.6ft) wide and 26 meters (85ft) tall - making it the largest fountain in Rome. The fountain dates back to ancient Roman times - actually to the construction of the Aqua Virgo Aqueduct in 19 B.C. that provided water to the Roman baths and the fountains of central Rome.

The fountain was built at the end point of the aqueduct, at the junction of three roads. These three streets (*tre vie*) give the Trevi Fountain its name, the Three Street Fountain.

The myth or charm of the fountain is the belief that there is magic here. This originated in 1954 with the movie, "Three Coins in the Fountain." The myth is as follows:

- If you throw one coin into the fountain: you will return to Rome

- If you throw two coins into the fountain: you will fall in love with an attractive Italian

- If you throw three coins into the fountain: you will marry that person that you met

This is why people are always throwing coins into the water. And, in order to achieve the desired effect of the coin throwing, one should throw the coin with their right hand over their left shoulder.

If you come to Rome, we wish you luck! And love!

On our way back to the Villa Borghese, we make sure we take a short detour just north of the Trevi Fountain to admire the gorgeous Spanish Steps or *Scalinata di Spagna.*

The Steps are one of the biggest tourist draws in Rome.

The Spanish steps were designed by an unknown architect called Francesco de Sanctis as a gift to Rome. They were built between 1723-1725. There are one hundred thirty-eight steps with various vistas over the Eternal City. They are a great example of Roman Baroque style architecture.

I think that the one thing everyone must do in Rome is climb the 138 stairs of the Spanish Steps to the top. Even with there being this many stairs, each step is shallow, and the climb is broken up by terraces where you can stop and catch your breath if needed. Easy enough! On top of the stairs, you will find many artists. So, you can have your portrait drawn here, be it a caricature or classic.

At the bottom of the steps, on the surrounding streets, you can find many of Rome's most exclusive temples to high fashion - including Fendi, Bulgari (which paid for a recent renovation of the Spanish Steps), and Valentino. Other iconic names in Italian fashion, such as Prada, Gucci, and Armani, are also close to the steps!

After all our sightseeing and being worn out and overheated from the sun beating down on us, Texel and I decided she would swim. We headed back to the park of the Villa Borghese. I must now confess that we have to *sneak* to have her swim in a fountain because it is not only illegal in the Trevi Fountain, but in all the fountains. We two villains were all set for another great adventure this sunny day in Rome.

So, off we were to find a suitable fountain for her to have some fun in. Texel is never picky about where she swims, but she is clueless of the chance we take sneaking around.

The fountain we chose is called la Fontana dei Cavalli Marini - The Water horses. It is astoundingly beautiful and made of carved horses that have the bodies of horses with fish tails. It is an architectural masterpiece. Every time I pass it, it amazes me as I soak up the beauty of the fountain.

The fountain is a large round structure with the horses in the center - the water comes from between the front legs of the horses and the top of the center filling the large round basin with fresh water. Texel loves to take a dip.

As I mentioned, since swimming in the fountains in Villa Borghese is illegal, I had to be on the lookout for Vigili - AKA Meter Maids - who are now, politically correctly called Parking Enforcement Officers!!!

We wanted to have fun, and, since we do not have a pool or lake near our home and cannot resist, we take our chances at the fountain. Trying to do something we know we should not be and not being caught is exciting, however, if the Vigili catches your dog in the fountain, the fine can go up to 450 Euro. (over $505.00 US dollars)

Everyone knows Golden Retrievers are avid water dogs. They will swim anywhere they can find water; even puddles on the road after a rain. I consider them fish with fur.

So, to continue with our adventure, on this particular day we snuck into the fountain for a swim. I was diligently on look-out duty for the Meter Maids as Texel enjoyed her swim. She jumped over and over in the water and played; frequently catching the jets of water in her mouth. Sometimes, she dove head first into the water and then leaped in the air as she came up out of the water.

She is a site for sure.

After about thirty minutes of exuberant fun, and, just as I was about to call her out of the water, I was stopped by the Vigili. Ugh.

They informed me of what I was already aware - that I was not allowed to let my dog swim in the fountain and they intended to give me a ticket.

With some fast thinking, I started playing the innocent foreigner routine. Using very bad Italian like a tourist would, I told them I did not know she was not allowed to swim here. It was so beautiful that I thought she was allowed.

Both Vigili (police) were men, and I feel a bit badly saying it, but I find Italian men are easily persuaded by feminine charm.

I played my innocent part well, so well they let me go without a ticket. Every now and then I see them in the park. We wave, nod, and smile. Sometimes I wonder if they figured out I am not a tourist, but an Italian now.

Let me tell you that, because Rome has so many tourists, this has worked for me when stopped for driving too fast and other jams I get myself into as well as allowing my dog to swim in the fountains. Don't try this in Holland though, they don't seem to fall for it.

And, for the record, every bit of this story is true!

Chapter 5

PICNIC IN THE PARK- THE INTERRUPTION

As we did on many days, Texel and I jumped in the car and went to Villa Borghese for a beautiful day's walk in the dog park where Texel is still allowed off the leash.

We were enjoying our day thoroughly until the moment, in my opinion, Texel found a dirty old tennis ball covered with drool. It was one of those balls that twenty-five other dogs already had in their mouths, and, to make matters worse, looked like it must have been sitting in the mud for days.

Texel, however, did not find it the least bit disgusting; so we played fetch. It was the usual game where I kicked the disgusting ball, she ran after it, and after retrieving it, returned it to me to play again.

Each time I kicked the ball, large amounts of drool and dirty slobber splashed all over. I thought it was the ghastliest ball ever, but she was enjoying herself immensely!!! Dogs!!!!

When she tired of the game, after what seemed an eternity to me, we began our jaunt through the park. Still off the leash in the dog park, we walked near the Silvano Toti Globe Theatre; commonly known as the Shakespeare Theatre.

While it is considered by some to be an imitation of the world famous London Globe Theater - a theater no one could copy - it is a new place, all Italian, and in line with safety regulations; to guarantee ideal conditions for the public. I am certain it has all the charm of the London Globe.

The beauty and charm of Rome is due not only in its historic, artistic heritage but also in contemporary works like the

Silvano Toti Globe Theater that confirm and renew the image of Rome as a capital of world culture.

With that in mind, the addition of the Silvano Toti Globe Theater took place at a particularly significant moment for Rome. It was the time celebrating the 100th anniversary of Villa Borghese in 2003. This Elizabethan theater seemed to merge Rome with the city of London, home of the famous Globe Theater.

This amazing culture is brought right into the city of Rome - into the Villa Borghese. The theater was built with wood from forests managed and reforested and has been perfectly inserted in the environmental and cultural context of Villa Borghese.

The theater is made as a circular structure and the roof is turned out; there is also the classic rectangular stage with a shed. It is as charming as can be seen in the photo.

Have you ever longed to experience movies such as *Shakespeare in Love* played out live and in person at an

Elizabethan theater? Well, that dream is possible. For a few euros you can go back in time!

Viewers can sit on the ground in front of the stage as did the people at the times of London and Shakespeare. You can also sit in the audience like a true lord! If you choose to sit on the ground, remember to bring a pillow, but, if you forget, no problem; you can always rent one at the theater for only a small fee of a mere 1.50 euros. Many of the visitors do.

Every theater lover can see plays like *The Merchant of Venice* and *A Midsummer's Night* to name just a couple. All plays are performed in Italian. Only the last play of the season is performed in English. This is exactly why Rome is a city, but it has the culture of a village and the main reason people do not move from here.

Rome is a unique place carved out in the world around us. Texel and I are so amazed each time we walk by.

And, as we walked on, my admiration for the Theater still swirling thoughts around in my mind, my attention was drawn to a couple sitting on one of the nearby benches kissing passionately. *'Oh, to be young again,'* I thought....

However, the closer we came, the more apparent it became that this couple were well in their late forties. What a surprise to Texel and me!

It is very unusual to see couples being so romantic in public, but, after all, this *is* a very romantic city. They seemed to be very happy. Love is in Rome, that's for sure.

As we approached, I spotted the picnic basket Texel spotted light years before I did. Not only are retrievers water dogs, they are chow hounds - always leading with their stomachs and noses.

All is great with Texel until she picks up the scent of something in the air; and she did again today. Suddenly, her nose pointed straight up and her tail pointed straight behind her. Her 'retriever' stance. In pursuit of sandwich!

"OH, NO!" I thought!!! Texel was still off leash.

I have come to the unfortunate conclusion that Texel only gets excited when she can cause havoc. As we came closer to the couple, she locked her nose into her 'scent' mode and began running toward the picnic basket and, as always, I ran after her. I just know I look silly when this happens.

I screamed her name like a banshee; all the while being careful not to break my neck or be run over by the many militant mountain bikers riding their bicycles in all directions around us!!!

Texel made it to the picnic basket before I could catch her. No surprise there. Her interest was with what was inside, of course. She passed the couple and, when she arrived at the basket, she dropped the disgusting drooling ball right into the basket, picked out the sandwiches, and ran off!

It all happened so fast no one had a chance to react. However, it only took seconds for the woman to start screaming; interrupting their passionate kiss!!!!

The man obviously wanted his 'misses' to see he was a strong and sturdy man, so, as was our usual reception and response to Texel's behavior, he proceeded to scream at me and Texel!!!

Casanova yelled, "Put your dog on the leash!!!"

I responded to his boisterous command in a heightened voice of my own. "No, this is a dog park!!!" Afterwards, I wished I had done things differently. It really wasn't their fault my dog has bad manners and unfortunate habits.

I tried to be apologetic and wanted to offer to get them sandwiches in the Zoo bar just up the hill, but, before I could, the man I call Casanova, continued to yell. He was not only yelling, he was saying some very 'not very nice' words, "%&^*@! ^, with your sandwiches, you and your dog!!!" he screamed.

This, I have to admit, made me change my mind about being nice and replacing the sandwiches. I wish things had gone differently, but they did not. I tried to do the right thing.

In the meantime, Texel enjoyed her new found lunch with gusto. It's almost as if she smiles when she does these things.

We always seem to end a beautiful day with another episode of the havoc Texel causes.

I sure hope they find it in their hearts to forgive my girl and me. We really meant no harm – again.

Chapter 6

WORK-OUT IN THE DOG PARK

Villa Ada is another wonderful park in Rome Texel and I visit. It is in the Northeastern section of the city and is close to the northern part of Villa Borghese. It has a spacious landscape over an area of 450 acres (1.8 km^2).

The wild expanse contains both public and private areas. The public area is controlled by the Council of Rome and is much larger than the private area.

Villa Ada contains an artificial lake and many trees, including many we call Stone Pines, Holm Oaks, Laurels and a very rare Metasequoia, which was imported from Tibet in 1940.

Entrance to the park is free and for a day of fun, one may rent canoes or bicycles. There is also a large swimming pool. There are many fun things to do here.

Since 1994, during the summers, the park hosts the world-music festival and the Liberation Project 2019 at Villa Ada against racism, war and the death penalty. Both are rather enjoyable.

One of the things I love most about Villa Ada is it has a great dog park. The other areas of the park are used for picnics, playing games, and jogging. It seems everyone loves the Villa

Ada, but my experiences are leading me to believe that some silly (in my opinion) visitors do not seem to love dogs.

Today we visited the 'dog' pond, played together, I drank cappuccino, and then we decided we were tired and headed to the car to go home. It always seems my fun time with Tex passes quickly.

As we made our way to our car, we walked through the entire dog park again - in reverse. We enjoyed all the same sights and sounds we did when we first came. We seemed to have escaped the day without any mishaps and all was perfect, so I spent a few minutes reading messages on my mobile phone.

Suddenly, I looked up and realized Texel was gone. One would think with all this area, and being tired, Texel could manage to avoid havoc; but not my dog.

Just a little way away, I saw three men exercising. Texel saw them first, of course. Now, I asked myself, what is more appealing to a puppy - coming to the car to go home with me with my arms waving like a maniac in the air, screaming for her to come or running off to meet three potentially new friends? It's a no-brainer with a Golden and, yes, she chose to meet new friends.

Now, I am not the fashion police, but these three men were wearing what I considered the most hideous sports clothes; clothes I think should be forbidden by law! They were so bright that even the wildlife moved to another side of the park when they neared!!! To make my point more emphatically, they lit up the area all around them. No one could possibly miss them. Point made!

"God help me," I thought. Since we were in the dog park area of Villa Ada, and dogs were permitted off leash, I did not feel a need to run full speed to retrieve my Retriever. I felt justified in feeling the men had the entire Villa Ada at their disposal and they were technically invading our space. I asked myself, "Why did they have to exercise in the dog park?"

It wasn't long before I heard them screaming "Signora, il suo cane ha rubato un guanto." (translated - 'madam, your dog has stolen a glove') So, I casually walked up to Texel and them.

After a huge struggle - because Texel saw this little 'pulling on the glove' as playtime - I managed to pull the glove from Texel's mouth. I handed it back to its owner. One second after I removed the one glove, my mischievous dog took the other glove!!!

"Bad girl," I scolded.

Not only did she grab the second glove, she ran away with it; refusing to give it to me.

There I am, if you can imagine it, running full speed after my dog with the sporty men shouting at me to get my dog. What did they think I was doing? They didn't even offer help. Looking back on it all, I should have caught my dog and left.

After a few minutes, a long hike around the park, and out of breath, I lost my patience. "Get my dog?! You do realize you are in a dog park?!" I barked at all three of the men.

"This is not a dog park," one indignantly informed me.

All three men watched as I ran in circles like a circus clown. I was red in the face, gasping for air, and my hair was disheveled. They must have been amused because they struck up conversation with me and asked, "Where are you from?"

"I live in Rome and where I am from is none of your business!!!" I shouted back. This was all I could think to say because I was livid.

Next, I heard mumbling, "Why doesn't she go back to her own country?" This question always makes me so angry I see red.

Like spitting poison, I responded, "If all the Italians living in my country returned to Italy, I would gladly go back to my own country." I didn't really mean it, I was just frustrated and angry.

As we continued quarrelling, Texel's next trick was "nicking" (a British way of saying 'stealing') one of the men's sunglasses.

I knew we were in serious trouble when she did this and this would be 'WAR.' One should never come between an Italian and his clothes or accessories!!! He went ballistic.

He screamed, "These are very expensive sunglasses. You will have to pay for them."

To which I responded, "Absolutely not, you are in a dog park; exercise somewhere else!"

He continued, insisting, "This is not a dog park!!!"

I shouted back, "No? Shall I call the Vigili so *they* can tell you this is a dog park??!!!"

Dismissing all I had to say, he continued, "You have to reimburse me for the damage!!!"

I replied, "Here is my name and telephone number, but how do I know these glasses are expensive?!"

He informed me, "These are Wayfarer Sunglasses and cost 170 €." (over 190 USD)

I was shocked and frustrated and insulted him when I said, "I would have to play the lottery to pay for those. Plus, they look like you bought them in a tourist shop!!!" As I mentioned, I am not very fashion aware and I blurt out things I later regret when upset or taken by surprise.

"@%*!#*" was what he spouted back to me.

And so I did just what he ordered me to!!! With Texel on the lead and my head up high, but shaking in my shoes, I marched to my car.

Later that afternoon I checked my social media page and, low and behold, there was a message from the goon in the park. The man found me. "Goodness, social media is determined to ruin my life," I thought. I asked the universe for some help here.

He sent a receipt of the damaged glasses. I humbly wrote back apologizing for the events of the day and said I could contribute 50 €. He agreed to accept this amount and I thought that was that. BUT NOOOOOOO!!!!!

He wrote again asking where I am from and if I would be interested in attending one of his concerts; seems he is a musician. I told him I am married and my husband surely would not appreciate my attending his concert.

"Put that in your designer jacket," I thought. I never heard from him again. Texel and I survived another challenging event!

Chapter 7

SHOPPING TROLLEY
THOUGHTLESSNESS

Texel and I live in the Southeastern area of Rome in a small, but well-known area called San Lorenzo. When I first came to Rome, I did not want to be here because there were graffiti everywhere. This spelled 'bad area to live in' to me since all the places I have lived, *only* the 'bad' areas of town had graffiti. This made me afraid. But I learned this is not so here.

To make matters worse, I was promised a lovely and breath-taking apartment near the Colosseum by my mother-in-law, but she denies ever having promised it to us.

Since moving to San Lorenzo I have grown to love it. This is 'my little neck of the woods.' I have become part of the community here.

San Lorenzo was an impoverished area at one time. Most of the apartments here were built for the rail track workers because San Lorenzo is close to the Termini train station. Also, because rent was low, the area attracted many artists. The area actually became famous because of the artists who made it a left-wing area to this day - an attribute that means you care for people. As with everything in Italy, even politics are considered fashionable.

But, with fame, came change; now the rent is higher and most of the artists have left. Developers have created loft style apartments out of the studio style apartments and they sell for what I consider a small fortune.

Even with the changes, the spirit of San Lorenzo is still alive; we all know each other, if not by name, by face. This gives me a deep feeling that I belong here. Most people have a nickname. I am known as the l'Olandese. (the Dutch woman). My neighbor is called BuBu. Why? I have no idea. We all feel so much like family here.

Many Romans come to San Lorenzo to eat because the restaurant kitchens are still authentic. San Lorenzo is filled with pubs, bars, and restaurants. I have to say I have no one favorite restaurant; I have many favorite restaurants. There is 'La trattoriola di Luca' on Via Tiburtina 8 that cooks authentic Roman food; it is tiny and busy, so a reservation is advised.

For pizza, I think 'Formula Uno' on Via Degli Equi' 13 Roma serves the best pizza in Rome. The pizza is delicious and the prices very good. All the ingredients are fresh every day. This is one of the places where you can still order a 'quartino' di vino - a quarter liter of wine.

They also have the most amazing starters (appetizers) like Baccali Fish - a deep fried stock-fish, and deep fried mozzarella balls I know everyone would enjoy.

They serve sweet and sumptuous melon when it is in season. The only thing is they do not take reservations, you just have to wait in line; which can be quite long.

'Formula Uno' is a bit of a big, loud place and, the moment you finish your pizza, you are expected to leave because there is always a line of people waiting for a table; it is worth the wait though. The pizzas are not only delicious; they are reasonably priced. At ca. 7 Euro (7.87 USD) each, you can't lose. 'Yum!' I love to talk about food!

If you want to eat pizza and pasta in a calmer environment, 'Ristorante Pizzeria I Fratelli,' Via degli Umbri, 14/18, 00185 Roma serves Neapolitan Pizza. This pizza is the same as the Roman pizza when it comes to toppings, but the difference is that the Neapolitan pizza has a thicker and softer base. In addition to pizza, they offer pasta and meat dishes. I highly recommend the Pasta Cacio e Pepe. Cacio is a dish I mention later in this book.

After all this talk about food, I am ready for lunch, but today Texel and I were not having lunch. We decided to walk in our lovely neighborhood. As we started out our door, we made our first stop at a 'rummage around' in an Outlet Store below our apartment.

I have never purchased anything here, but they have great deals including gorgeous coats by all the prominent designers like Valentino and Dolce e Gabanna. They are discounted from 1,500 Euro (1686.82 USD) to 700 Euro (787.18 USD) and, even though this is a fantastic offer - over 1/2 off - it is still too much money for me on my limited budget. I love to shop and, as we all know, looking is free. Plus, as an added bonus, I am able to have a chat with the owner of the Outlet Store. He knows all the goings on in the neighborhood and enjoys bringing me up to date on all the latest gossip and the goings on in the streets around us.

Also, there is another store I enjoy visiting; a fantastic pottery shop that is on the same street as my apartment. They sell lamps, plates, vases and more. I find their creativity stunning.

It is good go have a map like the one above. As Texel and I continue down our street, we turn right and pass various bars and a delightful old fashioned grocery shop that carries the

61

most delicious cheeses, sliced meats, and bread. I often stop to buy goat cheese with peppers. This is so delicious with a good glass of wine. Scrumptious! It also makes me sentimental, as my parents had a shop similar to it in Holland.

A bit further along, a lady recently opened a shop with children's clothing. I am not certain how I woke up one morning and am suddenly an 'old aunt' when I am not old by any stretch of the imagination; but my nephew had a baby. I guess that makes me the 'old aunt' much to my objection.

I often stop to look at the cutest handmade baby clothes. I bought my niece a darling little dress that said 'sono la principessa di mamma e papa.' (I am mommy and daddy's princess)

They also sell crocks for babies. Now, I will never be seen in my crocks outside, but these ones for babies were just too cute for words. I had to buy them even if she would never wear them.

We enjoy every minute of shopping and treating ourselves to delicious food.

The Immaculata church in the center of San
Lorenzo

Continuing our walk in the neighborhood, we come to
the church Santa dell' Immacolata. This church is wonderful and
helps so many. They help families with all the local funerals and
the nuns cook meals for the homeless. Every day at 11 am the
homeless can go to the church and get a plate of pasta, bread,
fruit and a bottle of water.

Most use this church rather than the Basilica San
Lorenzo Fuori le Mura because it is much smaller. We often
joke about the Santa dell' Immacolata because we have never
seen a wedding in the church, just funerals. There are many
activities around the small church though.

It is always a busy place.

San Lorenzo is a very political area and I feel this is because the University is located next to San Lorenzo, with the faculty of psychology in San Lorenzo. Italy is a very confusing country when it comes to politics; we have over forty political parties - and they all have their own 'fashion.' (ideas)

This may seem absurd to Americans because for me - a Dutch woman - it seems absurd. But this is the way it is in Rome, Italy. I always smile and tell my husband the students are left wing until they get their degree, then they become right wing. (The left is socialism and communism - more of democratic view and the right is capitalistic and materialistic - more of a republican view.)

I think the University students are idealistic and most of the students' bills are paid by their parents. That being so, I feel they have little knowledge about what real life is all about as I hear them sing songs from the '60s. They voice how they are great believers in change. I love them for this because it keeps me young and reminds me of my own younger, carefree days when I thought I could change the world.

On the square before the San Lorenzo Immaculata church is the Piazza dell' Immacolata. It is a large bar where I meet my posse of girlfriends once a week. We have a great time and drink coffee, gossip, and discuss politics. They are a lovely group of women and are some of the creative people in San Lorenzo. There are many painters, sculptors, and actors and actresses in my little area. My posse consists mostly of designers and painters.

On the side of the Santa dell' Immacolata church is a market square that has enticing fresh fish and vegetables and fruit from the land. They only sell what is in season, so it is guaranteed to be fresh. I buy here often and many tourists like to come here as well because of the freshness and selection that can be found here in this lovely market.

Next to the food section of the market is the open market where every day a shopper can discover different stands selling vintage clothes, shoes, earrings and clothes. I love to shop here.

I always hear the sellers shouting out 'Made in Italy,' however, when I look at the stitching, I know it was made in China or Vietnam. I don't mind this and I always buy my clothes at the market.

I recently bought a gorgeous second hand 'Guess' bag and a mean pair of snake leather boots that were also second hand and only paid 30 Euro. (33.71 USD)

I sometimes have difficulties with sizes in Italy because I am a north European and am 5 feet '8 inches tall; which makes me a giant compared to the average Italian. Most of the time I am successful at finding clothes to fit me.

If I buy blue jean pants, I make sure I try them on to check the fit. I do so at my friend's perfumery shop on the corner. Tops are never a problem to fit and, for 5 euro each, I just love shopping for them at the market.

Even though the prices may be low, I have still learned to haggle. There was a time I was too embarrassed to haggle, but now I am a master at negotiating! I know most of the stall (booth) holders and they enjoy playing this 'game' with me.

On our way to Il Verano, we turn right onto Via Tiburtina, but, first we must stop at the animal shop. Texel always finds a treat there and she refuses to continue until I get her just that right treat.

Across the road is the park of the Fallen where a monument stands to honor the inhabitants of San Lorenzo and as a memorial of WWII.

As we continue our walk, we find Villa Mercede on the corner of Via Tiburtina and Via dei Ramni. Here, there is a lovely park that does not allow dogs, but houses a library.

Libraries in Italy are different from England, Holland and, I also believe, the United States. In villa Mercede, you are allowed to read the books, but only in the library. No one is permitted to take the books home, read them, and bring them back as some are accustomed to.

At Villa Mercede, we cross the road again. I cross because I can't seem to pass a bar called 'C'era una volta' (Once Upon a Time) without enjoying my 90-euro-cent (1 USD) cappuccino and a cornetto.

This bar makes their own pastries and the smell alone is so irresistible it forces you to order a pastry that is deliciously fresh. You may have to wait for a table, but it is worth it.

From here I can see 'Il Verano' - the cemetery. The Campo Verano (Italian: Cimitero del Verano) is Rome's foremost cemetery. The cemetery is currently divided into sections: the Catholic cemetery, the Jewish cemetery, and the monument to the victims of World War I.

We cross Via dei Rieti to arrive at the cemetery. The shops nearby sell ornamental decorations for the families to place on their loved ones' graves. I sometimes visit these shops because I have a soft spot for angels; and they have a lovely selection.

I often walk Texel at the Cemetery Verano. I know it sounds morbid, but it is so beautiful and quiet. This is a great contrast to most of Rome. Don't get me wrong, Rome is gorgeous and has a fantastic history and many things to enjoy, but it is also extremely noisy.

On our way back home, I remembered I needed some things from the supermarket. It was still early in the morning, but had already warmed up and, since we were already out, I decided to take Texel with me; this seemed easier than walking home, leaving her, and going out again.

Some people love supermarkets. I hate them with a PASSION!!!! I hate the way people block the small aisles and carefully inspect the different cheeses on display. Aaahhhh!!!!

Another of my pet peeves is the till (the cashier). There is always a long line of people and only one till open, so you stand in the queue (the line) for what seems like forever and become more and more frustrated. And don't get me started on what I call the 'evil oldies' who think just because they are old, they can "queue hop" without asking.

When I first arrived in Rome, I didn't say anything to the little ladies because everyone knows it is expected conduct to 'respect the elderly.' In Italy, however, if you think like that, you will never get home. I have decided that the older people are, the more cunning they seem to become. No meanness intended.

Anyway, back to Texel and me. Since I was not able to take her inside the market and wanted to keep her safe, I clipped her leash to one of the shopping trolleys (aka shopping carts in America).

The shopping trolleys are always attached to each other. I made sure I was careful to clip her leash on a trolley in the middle to avoid trouble.

As a rule, I do not like doing this because it makes me very nervous. I am usually very careful with my girl.

Today, the first and the last carts were not attached to each other and all the trolleys in between. This was a recipe for disaster ahead; one I was not able to predict.

I thought she would be safe if I left her for the short time it would take me to gather a few items. As I walked away, however, it was only minutes until I heard the desperate barking that shortly became howling after which I soon heard rise to the level of severe consternation.

I dropped my shopping items and ran to the tills where, through the window, I saw Texel running over across the road with three shopping trolleys attached to her leash. All the trolleys were *not* connected; it was just my luck!!!

Without looking, and, with no regard for my safety, I ran across the road after her. I stopped on-coming cars with my hand as I ran after Texel. I thought later, 'What a great traffic controller I could be.' No time for nonsense now, though, my precious girl was petrified and did not understand. She did not realize she was attached to the trolleys; she thought she was being chased.

Finally, I caught up to her and quickly freed her from the trolleys; all danger behind us. The kind people from the supermarket took the trolleys back to the store for me as I took Texel in my arms and promised her I would never leave her again or attach her to shopping trolleys! We were both shaking, but we knew we were okay.

This was a most horrifying experience for both of us!!! When I was able to process my thoughts, I realized how lucky we were I was able to stop the cars in the street and neither of us were hit. I am also happy the trolleys did not damage any parked cars or injure my Texel.

Since it is a small community, naturally everyone heard about our day at the supermarket. And still, to this day, people stop me on the street and ask, "Is she the dog that went running with the shopping trolleys?"

I answer with a heart filled with a mixture of gratitude and guilt, "Yes, this is her!!!"

I always make sure I have enough time to get home with my little girl before I venture out to shop for food. We never want to make that mistake again.

Chapter 8

THE TOURISTS

At times, I prefer to avoid driving in the crazy Roman traffic, so I take Texel to a small nearby park in San Lorenzo.

The park we visit when I don't feel like sitting in traffic is 'Il Parco dei Caduti, (the park of the fallen in WWII). I may have mentioned it in a prior chapter.

In the park of the Fallen is a monument to the Fallen. The full name is 'Il Monumento ai Caduti del 19 luglio 1943.' (The monument of the fallen of 19th July 1943)

Although every person born in San Lorenzo feels strongly about the bombardment in WWII, very little is done to keep the Statue clean.

Since many dog owners take their dogs to this park, we have decided to collect 2 Euros (2.25 USD) a week from whoever wants to participate in donating. With the donations, we hire a person to keep the park clean and tidy.

Once a year a ceremony for remembering is held by the mayor of Rome who comes and places a wreath at the monument in memory of all those lost. This is lovely, however, the monument is pretty much ignored the rest of the year.

Another lovely and famous landmark built near the park is the Basilica. This beloved church - Basilica San Lorenzo Fuori le Mura (San Lorenzo outside the wall) - is near a road called Via Tiburtina - a main road in Rome.

The basilica was built in the 14th Century and was badly damaged during the Second World War during the first Allied bombing of Rome.

After the war, the basilica was rebuilt and restored with the original material and completed in 1948, however, the ancient paintings of the upper part of the front of the church were unable to be restored.

This church is an important one to San Lorenzo because San Lorenzo is the Italian and Spanish name for Saint Lawrence, a 3rd-century Christian. Lawrence was among the seven deacons of the Roman church serving Pope Sixtus II whose martyrdom preceded Lawrence's by a few days. They were executed during the persecution of Christians under the Roman emperor

Valerian. It is said that Lawrence gave the church's treasures to the poor and the sick before his arrest.

A beautiful Sculpture of Saint Lawrence was created by Bernini between 1615 and 1618. The sculpture is not in San Lorenzo where he was martyred, but is held in the Uffizi Gallery in Florence.

Within the Parco dei Caduti (park of the fallen) is a coffee shop and a children's playground. We often visit the coffee shop for a cappuccino and a cornetto.

The word cappuccino, I have come to realise, actually comes from the word "capuchin" which means hood. The foam is the 'hood' of the coffee. A cornetto is the Italian version of the French croissant. The difference is the cornetto is sweet and the croissant is savoury. I simply cannot resist these.

I hope you can see how San Lorenzo is an area that grows on you. As I mentioned before, when I first arrived with my Italian husband, I told him, "I am not going to live here." The walls were full of graffiti. In England and Holland, places you see graffiti are usually not the safest neighborhoods.

The reason there is so much graffiti is because we still have groups that call themselves communists, or even anarchists; something the rest of Europe dealt with in the 1970's. Somehow, Italy cannot unite and therefore forms small, independent groups in order to 'belong.' Each group finds it necessary to spray their groups' 'symbol' on walls.

In countries like America there are two political parties - democrats and republicans. In Italy, we have over 40 parties and this can get a bit tricky as I think anyone can see and makes things slightly more confusing at times.

I have learned that San Lorenzo is a very left wing area, but it has the warmth of taking people into the community and accepting them for who they are. Even as a person who did not grow up here, I feel much loved in my little San Lorenzo; I feel a sense of home. Since my first impression of San Lorenzo, I have gained much understanding of Italy's political structures. What I cherish about Italy has nothing to do with politics and everything to do with the people who have welcomed me and treat me as if I am one of their own. For this, I am grateful.

San Lorenzo is also a very interesting area because there is a mixture of people born here and still live in the same house and students who come to enjoy their new 'freedom.'

Everyone is excited when I say I am from the Netherlands. They immediately talk about, tulips, wooden shoes, and other things peculiar to the Netherlands.

Whenever I visit my home town in Holland, I make sure to bring back key holders with little wooden shoes to hand out to my friends.

I feel very accepted, but feel it has somewhat to do with the fact that I am Dutch; I come from a small but rich country. Therefore, the locals feel I 'fit in.' I know others sometime experience a more difficult time fitting in if they are not financially stable. I think people should accept everyone despite their financial status, but sometimes things happen I cannot seem to change.

Today, Texel and I played ball. While throwing her ball, I spotted the most colorful parade to have ever seen enter the park. It was as though we had traveled back in time and arrived in the 1980s. The people in the parade wore big and teased hair, big hats and big shoulder pads. As I was distracted and enthralled with this group and the parade, Texel decided on staring at a different group of people at the coffee shop.

Now, Texel and I share the same vice; *the cornetto* (the Italian croissant)!!! I can manage to control myself, however, whenever she smells one, she will do anything in her power to steal one.

The coffee shop has cornetti and cakes delivered every day. The tourists staying at a hotel across from the park are offered breakfast in the coffee shop. Even though Texel was not a hotel patron, she was off to see what she could get.

I ran after Texel - as usual. I arrived at the outdoor seating area where a loud commotion was going on. The women were screaming; some of them climbed onto their chairs. One of them even dove into the bushes surrounding the small terrace. It was crazy; to say the least.

As soon as I could make sense of all the commotion, I discovered Texel stole a cornetto and, knowing there were more for the taking, she refused to let me grab her!!! While ducking and diving around the tables to retrieve my misbehaving Retriever, I was suddenly stopped by a woman. She informed me - in a thick Russian accent - that I had to apologize to the woman whose cornetto Texel had stolen!!!

Since I was frantically trying to get my dog, initially I paid little attention to her. The only thing on my mind was getting hold of Texel before she stole more cornetti!!! Texel is a bit like an eel; just when you think you have her, she slips through your fingers.

After I finally grabbed hold of her, I turned to the woman whose cornetto had been stolen and apologized. I politely asked if I could buy her another one. I always do this, as it is very rude and sometimes scary for people when a dog bounces up and grabs something from you the way Texel does. This woman did not respond to my offer.

The woman who insisted I apologize, however, and, who I can only assume was the travel guide, stood and scolded me relentlessly. She told me I was a horrible woman!!!

While I realize different people respond differently in these situations, I find some people more dog friendly than others are in the same situation.

Exasperated, I did not know how to respond. I thought, "Couldn't they see I was frantically trying to collect my dog?" While I kept trying to apologize and make amends, she kept saying I was rude. I really did not think so. I was not casual or uncaring about what Texel had done and I offered to buy her another pastry. Texel is just a puppy - granted a big puppy.

It's easy to think bad thoughts at a time like this. I did. "*Silly moo,*" I thought. I tried to stay nice. I again told her I was very sorry about what had happened!!! To her this must have sounded something like "ç°/@]/)&/" because all of the sudden, she pushed me backwards.

I was startled and, when I regained my balance, I stood motionless. I could not believe what just happened.

Then, I received a sea of insults over me from this group of tourists. They continued until the owner of the coffee shop came out and told the guests they had to leave. It seems they had been extremely rude to him as well. They called him names and insisted they were entitled to extra coffee at no charge. He had enough of them. Usually tourists are a happy bunch.

I was happy to be rescued by him at this moment. Texel and I sure needed it.

The crowd ignored the owner of the shop and refused to stop shouting until a police car arrived. It was only then that the group calmed down.

The police just happened to be stopping to take a coffee, but the tourists thought they were there because of them. They transformed into a group of calm and charming ladies and even flirted with the policemen.

I admit this episode scared me. I have never been pushed like that before and was not expecting it. Texel must have sensed my upset because as we walked home, she walked closely to me like a trained police dog!!! My great girl - even if the tourists did not think so.

One can never be too careful in this world. Usually tourists are so happy to see all the sites in Rome they are kind and polite. This is not always the case. All ended well though for me and my girl.

We are sure glad for this. Rome is still a lovely place and we don't want anyone to get a wrong impression of our great home.

We are very careful around so many tourists now. We try to avoid the larger crowds.

Chapter 9

PONYTAIL PILVERING

Despite having many shops close to my home in San Lorenzo, I sometimes find it fun and exciting to go to the center of Rome to buy something not available in my area.

When I make the trip into the center of Rome, it also serves as an opportunity to help Texel adjust to the hustle and bustle of city life and gives her experience on the tram that leaves us in front of the Colosseum. We walk to various shops from there.

As usual, the area was crowded with tourists!!! There is always a lot of ooh-ing and aah-ing over Texel and numerous tourists take photos with her in front of the Colosseum!

At times she loves being the center of everyone's attention. I think she is beautiful and it makes me happy when others think so too.

We enjoy the sites in Rome as much as the tourists who come from everywhere to enjoy them. The Colosseum!

Rome's most popular monument was built between 72-80 A.D. It remains the largest amphitheater ever built, and stands as an iconic symbol of Rome.

The Colosseum was constructed as a gift to the Roman Citizens from the Flavian Dynasty to increase their popularity, to stage various forms of entertainment, and to showcase Roman engineering techniques to the world. It took approximately 60,000 Jewish slaves close to nine years to build! It is one of the Seven Wonders of the World. It is a must see for any tourist visiting Rome.

The Colosseum, whose real name is the Flavian Amphitheatre, named after the Flavian family line of Roman

Emperors, was given the name Colosseum because of a lovely statue located alongside the amphitheater called 'the colossus of Nero.'

In fact, the Roman Colosseum is always capitalized and spelled differently than the generic Coliseum. It is an oval amphitheater and it was built on a site chosen that is a flat area of a low valley between the Caelian, Esquiline and Palatine Hills.

The very first games at the Colosseum, held in 80AD by Emperor Titus, lasted for 100 days. There were over 3000 gladiator fights during them. The very last gladiatorial games were held in 435AD.

The Colosseum was built to hold an estimated 50,000 to 80,000 spectators; having an average audience of some 65,000. The design, consisting of 84 entry gates, allowed all the spectators to enter the theater in about 20 minutes and find their seats. The Romans claimed to have the earliest form of a sky dome; if it rained, they stretched a red canvas over the entire Colosseum!

Unfortunately, many natural disasters and stone-robbers devastated the structure of the Colosseum, but it was the earthquakes of 847 AD and 1231 AD that caused most of the damage seen today.

Despite all this, the Colosseum is still one of Rome's most popular tourist attractions. Interestingly enough, it also has close links to the Roman Catholic Church because each Good Friday the Pope leads a torch lit "Way of the Cross" procession that starts in the area around the Colosseum.

Also around the Colosseum, there are many green grassy areas where people come to jog or cycle; this is where Texel and I find enjoyment.

As usual in Rome, the area is busy. We have to dodge cyclists calling, "Passing," as they swiftly go by. Joggers are dressed in their unique outfits.

Texel and I found a place to sit in the rich luscious green grass that spread beneath us like a carpet. I kept Tex on the leash to avoid her usual havoc. We enjoyed all the business of Rome at that moment.

As we sat relaxing, I noticed a woman sitting on a yoga mat exercising. Further ahead, I spotted a far-eastern looking gentleman doing tai-chi. I could sit and watch this for hours because it is like a ballet to me rather than a martial art. I find it mesmerizing. Today, people were jogging in small groups.

Since we were close to the F.A.O. (which is the Food and Agriculture Organization) of the United Nations, there were many people speaking many languages to buy food here. This made me feel like I was in Biblical Babel because of the people speaking different languages all around me.

Also pleasurable were the birds chirping around us and we heard sea-gulls going to the roof terrace of the F.A.O. to find scraps at the restaurant there. The sea-gulls are easily pleased and always ready to eat whatever is served.

After a short rest, and, on our walk to some shops, Texel became interested in one particular female jogger. I happen to notice her as well. As I watched her, I mused about how envious I was because she was tiny and slim and with a very long ponytail.

I was envious because age has caught up with me in more ways than one. First of all, I am certain I would collapse or have a heart attack if I tried to jog any distance around the Colosseum. And, since I have two herniated discs in my back, running is the last thing I can do because the pain would be excruciating. Also, to top off the reasons for my envy, my hair isn't half as long as this jogger's!!! I was about to find out hers wasn't either.

As the lady passed, jogging at a moderate rate, Texel turned abruptly, nearly pulling me to the ground. Then, the dreaded moment came when I wished the earth would open so we could both disappear into oblivion as Texel jumped up at the lady's back and grabbed her ponytail!!!

Mixed emotions flooded my mind. I didn't know if I should laugh or cry!!! I began shouting at Texel to leave the hair, but the more emphatically I screamed, the more fun she seemed to be having.

I made a valiant effort to pry Texel's mouth open to remove the ponytail when the lady kindly said, "Don't worry, the hair is fake!!!"

Texel continued to engage in what she seemed to consider tug-of-war playing with the hairpiece. It soon became clear she and the ponytail had bonded like two lost siblings.

I turned to the lady with a sincere look of terror and apology on my face. She looked back and started laughing as she said, "Like I said, it's fake. It's not real hair, don't worry. She did no harm."

I offered to pay for the hairpiece. She said she wouldn't think of it. I could have kissed her for her sweetness because this could have ended badly. My dog not only stole her property and embarrassed her, she jumped up on her back and could have knocked her down. Sometimes we are lucky to meet such an understanding person.

Texel seemed to remember this day because afterward, for a couple of weeks, she jumped up at everyone with a ponytail; she did not care if it were a man or a woman. Most of the time I managed to control her and keep her down. Most people seemed too shocked to react to her behavior; many of them laughed. I am forever grateful for people who have a sense of humor and are patient with misbehaving dogs!

And I always say, "Dai, la vita è troppo breve," (Come on, life is too short!!!)

Chapter 10

LET'S GO AND SEE THE PONIES

This little story is about an adventure I had with Texel in another wonderful park in Rome we frequently visit called Villa Celimontana.

Villa Celimontana (formerly called the Villa Mattei) is a free public park that dates back to the sixteenth century. It is located on the western top of the Celio hill -one of the Seven Hills of Rome I briefly mentioned in the first chapter.

To orient us, Villa Celimontana is south of Trevi Fountain and situated between the famous Colosseum to the North and the enchanted Roman Baths (Terme di Caracalla) to the South.

Ah! The Roman Baths! Another amazing site in Rome.

The baths are a must see for any tour of Italy. They are truly ancient structures. They have been preserved after all these years and, sometimes look a little run down, but are certainly worth the visit.

The remains of the Baths of Caracalla were constructed between 212 and 216AD and are considered an architectural wonder of ancient times.

The baths had a sophisticated water supply, were heated with wood ovens built underground, had an elaborate drainage system, were covered with marble, and draped with valuable works of art. Lovely.

Visiting the baths was a beloved pastime for Roman citizens and visitors for over 300 years. They were closed in 537AD and, in spite of the passing of the centuries and of the lootings that the baths suffered, the ground floor of the buildings and a large part of the impressive walls that formed them remain.

By using your imagination, it is possible to submerge yourself in the splendor of ages past.

Our day today is in the park. Villa Celimontana is not a major tourist attraction; it is mainly used by the locals for a casual, quiet day out. Tourists may not even know it exists.

When Texel and I visit, we walk along winding paths through the trees and grassy areas and appreciate all the buildings, statues, flowers, and views.

Villa Celimontana is home to the Italian Geographical Society. This is an ethical group whose purpose it is to encourage the growth of geographical knowledge and scientific research.

Also, each year a jazz music festival is offered by the Villa Celimontana Cultural Association. Since the summer of 2012, an "I Classici in Villa" music festival has been held by the Alcatraz Association. Many other musical events are also enjoyed here.

There is a small pond in the park and many benches to sit either in the sun or the shade; all perfect locations for a picnic.

Sometimes we see families with young children enjoying a small play area. Other times we see a pony and cart taking children on rides around the park. There is also a pony ride area, but that is never open when we arrive at the early hour of 7 am.

We are sometimes surprised by green parrots who have made large nests in the park and by their impressive fuss! These green parrots are not native to Italy. They eat the food intended for birds that are native to Italy and so, sometimes, this makes them unwanted visitors.

The sign at the entrance bears graffiti, but thankfully there is none inside; nor any beggars, scarf sellers, selfie stick sellers etc etc. The park is a real place of tranquillity and one of our favourite places to visit.

Texel and I also love to watch the birds and butterflies and lizards. It is usually sooooo quiet; quiet in the middle of a very busy Rome.

We walk and enjoy this park for hours. We meet interesting people sometimes as well. Texel seems to enjoy our time here as much as I do.

The park has beautiful flower bushes and some interesting sculptures and is altogether quite lovely, yet a small park with a fountain big enough for Texel to enjoy a swim.

I am sure anyone can see why this park is one of our favourites. Since Texel and I are regulars in the Villa Celimontana, we know the other dogs and their owners who also frequent the park. This is nice because there is always someone to chat with.

One summer, the park organized a music festival and a bartender, who seemed to favour us dog-owners, '*opened*' the bar. It was heaven!!! I socialized while Texel played with the other dogs and, for one brief moment, it felt there was little she could do to give me anxiety!!! This was about to change.

Typically, Texel and I arrive early at the park in the summer because temperatures reach 40° C (104° F) with high humidity quickly. Today, our little group decided to walk around the park with our dogs and, after a time of being engrossed in conversation, I realized Texel was not with us. I frantically called her over and over, but no Texel.

One gentleman in the group called to me. I heard a giggle in his voice!!! *"What was he giggling about?"* I asked myself.

I ran to find Texel in the pony area. She found an opening in the fence and decided to roll around in the pony urine!!!! I am sure that those of you who know about pony urine can fully understand why I was repulsed!!!

Well, I had to get my girl. First, I climbed the fence with slight difficulty because I was wearing a dress that came above my knees and, as you can imagine, it is not easy to climb a fence in a short dress and keep one's poise.

When I finally caught her, she was dirty, wet from being covered in urine, and very smelly. I took her to the fountain and tried to rinse her as best I could!!! Just when I thought I was done, she escaped with her leash still on and darted right back to the pony area!!!

At this point, I felt like crying even though it was easier to catch her the second time because she was wearing her leash!!!! I decided to take her home immediately. Because I was so upset, I did not talk to her our entire drive back home!! I felt this a good punishment. I am not certain she received my message of upset though.

I am not exaggerating when I tell you my car smelled for an entire month!!!

We did not return to Villa Celimontana for the rest of the summer!!! That dog of mine!

Chapter 11

THE FLYING FORCE

Usually, I take Texel to a proper dog park because this avoids all sorts of trouble. Today, however, I felt like walking.

I decided we would walk to a special section of San Giovanni - an area within the walls of Rome about a 15- minute walk from our home.

I feel San Giovanni emanates the aura of "authentic Rome." The neighborhood is filled with older buildings, but does not have much of the city's notable cobblestone streets and low-lit wine bars.

San Giovanni has a 'local ambiance' and it has modern avenues that open out into breathtaking cathedrals. There are community produce markets rather than restaurants and entertainment happens in parks rather than clubs. San Giovanni invites tourists and modern Romans alike to see Roman history and the conveniences of the present day. I think this part of Rome is worth a little time if you are visiting.

San Giovanni is home to St. Giovanni in Laterano; which is the first Basilica of Rome. Basilica is the name given to churches in Italy. St. John Lateran is actually the official cathedral of Rome (not St. Peter's as most imagine) and is the seat of the Bishop of Rome – a.k.a. the Pope.

The famous St Peters Basilica is in the Vatican state – which is on the 'other side' of Rome from San Giovanni. The Vatican is unique in that it is a separate state – with their own mint, post office, and army.

Being one of the four major basilicas in Rome, the cathedral (St. Giovanni in Laterano) was built in the 4th century AD and is believed to be one the first Catholic churches in Rome.

Rome is a very religious city and most people, even if they do not attend mass, will walk into church and motion the sign of the cross to Jesus, almost a way of greeting Him.

Being a Protestant, I find the fact that a Catholic church is always open a nicety. And, although I was not raised Catholic, I do enter the church at times. I go mostly when I feel down, want some peace, or just want to sit and look at the beautiful frescos.

I always burn a candle for my late father. He wasn't Catholic, but for me it is my way of saying 'hello' to him. The atmosphere in the churches is very welcoming. They are very quiet, but you can tell, they gladly invite you in. This was especially meaningful to me for my times of remembering my dear father.

When I first arrived in Rome - in April some 15 years ago - it was Easter and someone knocked on my door. When I opened the door, there stood a priest with some holy water and palm leaves. He asked if I wanted my home blessed. I was so startled and taken aback by this the only thing I could say was, 'No thank you, I am Protestant.' I wish I had graciously accepted him as graciously as he offered God's blessing to me and my home and allowed him to bless our home.

I am certain that I will accept the next time someone offers me a special blessing. Tex and my husband and I need these things very much.

Ah! The Vatican City. I am miles away from Vatican City, but I think of it as I gaze upon the sites in my little area of San Giovanni. As I mentioned, Vatican City is a city within the city of Rome and on the other side of Rome from us. It is encircled by a 2-mile border within Italy. As an independent city-state, it covers just over 100 acres, making it one-eighth the size of New York's Central Park. Vatican City is governed as an absolute monarchy with the Pope at its head. The Vatican mints its own Euros, prints its own stamps, issues passports and license plates, operates media outlets and has its own flag and anthem.

At least four million Pilgrims - who are 'religious' tourists - visited the Vatican in 2016. Every Sunday, St Peters square is filled with worshippers.

Also present in Vatican City is the Swiss Guard. They are recognizable by their armor and colorful Renaissance-era uniforms. The Guard has been protecting the Pontiff (Pope) since 1506. The Swiss Guard's role in Vatican City is strictly to protect the safety of the Pope. And, yes, the force is entirely comprised of Swiss citizens.

One of the most famous and well-known buildings is still the Sistine Chapel; it is one of the most important treasures of the Vatican City of Rome and of the world in general. It is known as much for its embellishment as for being the temple in which Popes are chosen and crowned.

What grabs the interest in the Sistine Chapel is not its architecture, but the frescoes that entirely cover the walls and the ceiling. Some of the most significant artists who worked in the chapel are Botticelli, Perugino, Luca and, of course, Michelangelo.

Also a part of the Sistine Chapel in Vatican City, the Last Judgment earns special recognition. This fresco occupies the entire wall behind the altar of the Chapel and shows the final judgment of all humanity.

The Last Judgment in the Vatican is one of the main art works of Michelangelo. It took the great painter nearly four years to complete the fresco, a masterpiece that includes over 300 figures.

Apart from the Louvre in Paris, France, the world's best museums are the Vatican Museums. Located in the five hectare (Apostolic) Palazzo Apostolico Vaticano, the museums hold roughly 70,000 works of art, around which 20,000 are on display at any given time. If you were to spend just one minute looking at each work of art on display, you would be in the museums for roughly two weeks! Most tourists cannot devote that much time to one area of Rome.

Today, in San Giovanni by the St. Giovanni Laterano, everything was going well for Tex and me as we sat in the grass in front of the church, looking at the endless buses filled with tourists coming and going. With a little practice, anyone can tell immediately where the tourists are from. There are so many tourists each day.

For instance, at 20°C (68 °F), northern Europeans are typically dressed in shorts and T-shirts and the Italian and Spanish are typically dressed in warm jumpers and scarves. I am becoming rather good at guessing where the individual tourist is from; a little game I like to play. I don't mean to stereotype, just have fun.

Texel tried her usual trick of stealing food from the tourists, but I was grateful she had not succeeded!!! Her trick is to walk up to people with her tail wagging, then, when she gets their attention and affections, she quickly puts her nose in their bags to get what she can.

She has stolen glasses, maps, tickets; anything she can get her teeth into. Texel does not only do this here, she does it wherever she goes. I hope it is a puppy thing and that she will stop when she is an adult. Sometimes I find it very frustrating, but I love her too much to be too upset all the time.

I try my best to avoid these situations because non-dog lovers do not appreciate her antics, but the dog lovers find her charming and she uses this to the fullest for her own agendas.

Also, the usual photo opportunities for Texel with tourists present themselves frequently. These include 'Texel in front of the Basilica,' 'Texel sideways,' 'Texel with the whole family,' etc. And these are also opportunities for my young girl to cause havoc in Rome.

Usually, Texel really enjoys the pictures, however, I am not certain why, but occasionally Texel is not photogenic. When she refuses her usual modeling offers, I just smile and say, 'she has a Native American soul.' I tell others that, 'like the Native Americans, Tex is scared that by taking her photograph, her soul is taken.' Seriously, she will not sit still and pose. I always tell disappointed tourists that she has no ambition to become a supermodel. They smile and continue on.

As we sat enjoying all the sites and tourists, from out of nowhere, Texel jumped up and started growling!!!! *She never growls*, I thought. I tried to see what or who she was growling

110

at!!! For a moment, I did not understand why she was upset, but I soon discovered why and at that moment I was grateful I had not let her off her leash!!!

I looked all around but was unable to understand what was upsetting my silly animal. Then, I saw what Texel saw. She spotted a group of Catholic nuns dressed in their traditional habit. Oh, no! She never saw nuns before.

Nowadays, the headpiece to a nun's habit are smaller and the dresses simpler. Some nuns even wear jeans. In Rome, however, one usually never sees a nun in jeans.

When nuns and priests from all over the world visit Rome, their best Sunday outfits come out of storage. But these were very shocking; they were like the flying squad!!! These nuns were dressed in their traditional outfits; outfits so elaborate that even in Rome they caught the eye of everyone.

Texel surprised me with her reaction to the sisters as they walked by us. I did all I could to contain her. As I said, I am not Catholic, but Rome is a Catholic city and nuns and priests and monks are a part of the culture and everyday life here.

I have learned much about the nuns and their traditional dress.

Many years ago, a nun's 'uniform' was set to steep rules. The picture above is one from 1930. The habit may not be as strict as long ago, but still an important part of the nun's outfit to show respect for their faith. The uniform is:

The coif - (the garment's headpiece) is enormous.

Tunic: This is the central piece of the habit. It is a loose dress made of serge fabric pleated at the neck and drapes to the ground. It can be worn pinned up in the front or in the back to allow the nun to work.

Sleeves: The habit contains two sets of sleeves; the larger sleeve can be folded up for work or folded down for ceremonial occasions or whenever entering a chapel.

Underskirts: This complete vestment includes two underskirts, a top skirt of black serge trimmed with cord and a bottom skirt of black cotton.

Shoes: Simple functional black shoes are the usual footwear.

Nuns always carry these items:

A Cross: A cross of silver traditionally hangs from a black cord around the nun's neck.

A Ring: Nuns who have taken final or "perpetual" vows indicate this status by wearing a simple silver ring on the left hand.

A **Rosary**: The nun's rosary of wooden beads and metal links hangs from the belt by small hooks.

When she saw these nuns for the first time, Texel's growling turned to barking. Who could blame her? When I looked at all these ladies in a group, all these headpieces appeared like a ship coming into the harbor. It was overwhelming to me, so I could understand.

I must admit, however, that the other bystanders' response to Tex and I was not very pleasant or sympathetic to us!!! The bystanders treated me as if they thought my dog was rude to react to the holy sisters that way. She really did not know any better.

Ashamed, and with my head down, I dragged Texel away; repeatedly apologizing and saying to the people around us, "I am sorry, I am sorry."

Afterward, I felt I should not have had to apologize. My dog was just being a dog. She reacted this way to experiences that were new to her.

As we crossed the road back to San Lorenzo, it felt okay to smile again. Texel wagged her tail and greeted all the familiar folks in our neighborhood. We were home and safe and the people here would never be cross with her. She knew these people very well! And they like her.

Until this day, I am not sure what would have happened had Texel not been on the leash!!! We are glad we did not have to find out.

Chapter 12

TEXEL AND I AT THE PANTHEON AND PIAZZA NAVONNA

I decided to meet a friend one day for an 'aperativo.' (an aperativo is both an appetizer and a drink in Rome) 'Aperativi' usually starts at around 18:30 (6:30PM) and is similar to what some may know as happy hour.

At this particular time, the Spritz (prosecco, Aperol, and soda) is the fashionable light alcoholic drink. (Funny, even drinks are subject to fashion)

So, in anticipation of our great day, Texel and I took the nr 71 bus and as I looked at the clock, we were early, so I decided to walk to the Pantheon first. Off we were.

Today, almost 2000 years after its construction, the pantheon is breathtaking and an astonishing building to visit. It has been said that when Michelangelo saw the Pantheon for the first time, he said it is more like the work of angels, not humans.

The building is circular with enormous columns; an architectural wonder for sure. The 16 massive columns weigh 60 tons each. They are 39 feet (11.8 m) tall and five feet (1.5 m) in diameter.

The columns support a triangular pediment with an engraving assigning the Pantheon to Marcus Agrippa - ("M•AGRIPPA•L•F•COS•TERTIUM•FECIT" which means "Marcos Agrippa built it in his third consulate").

The word Pantheon is a Greek adjective meaning "honor all gods." It was first built as a temple to all gods. However, as times have changed, and since Rome is a Catholic city, it became 'fashionable' to have one god, so the Romans converted and became Christians. Now, the Vatican has taken over the Pantheon and it is no longer a 'church for all gods,' but a church for the Christian God.

The amazing part of the Pantheon is its enormous dome, with its renowned hole in the top - called the eye of the Pantheon, or oculus. The hole (oculus), 7.8 meters in diameter, is the only source of light into the building. Almost 2000 years after it was built, the dome remains the most magnificent unreinforced concrete dome in the world!

When I stand gazing up at the magnificent structure, I almost think it is God that is shining through to us here in Rome. I know this is silly, but I think very child-like sometimes. This hole allows rain to come in occasionally. The good thing is that the floor is slanted and the water drains well. It is truly a sight to see here in Rome.

The diameter of the dome is 43.30 meters or 142ft (compared to the United States Capitol dome which is 96 feet in diameter). The dome is in complete ratio with the Pantheon by the fact that the distance from the floor to the top of the dome is exactly equal to its diameter.

After our tour of the Pantheon, Texel and I made our way to Piazza Navona which is just a hop, skip, and a short way away to meet our friend for the aperativo we came for. Piazza Navona is one of the most charming and popular squares in Rome. It is one of my favorites.

For fun during Christmas, the entire Piazza is packed with market stands, children, games, and lots of different things to eat. Around that time, you will also see a witch on her broomstick.

The story goes that the three wise men were looking for Jesus and asked her the way. She, being a witch, told them she didn't know. After flying for a bit, she felt remorse and turned around to look for the three wise men. She could not find them. To live with her guilt, she comes around on January 6th each year and leaves sweets for all the children. This is a time for only sweets. Gifts are given at Christmas.

The area of the Piazza Navona is open with the square being enclosed by restaurants and terraces, which give the Piazza Navona a lively and friendly atmosphere during the day.

Here, visitors can enjoy performances by street artists like magicians and dancers and painters.

There are three magnificent fountains on the square that truly are what makes the Piazza so special.

Fontana del Moro

The Fontana del Moro was designed by Giacomo della Porta in 1575 with the dolphin and four Tritons. In 1653, the statue of the Moor, by Gian Lorenzo Bernini, was added. In 1874, during a restoration of the fountain, the original statues were moved to the Galleria Borghese and replaced with copies.

The Fontana dei Quattro Fiumi (Fountain of the Four Rivers) was designed by Bernini in 1651. The four figures represent the most significant rivers of the continents where Christianity had spread; the Nile, Danube, the Ganges and Rio de la Plata.

It is an amazing structure.

The Fountain di Nettuno

The Fountain di Nettuno is located at the northern end of the Piazza Navona. This fountain was given to Rome in 1574 and, as with the Fountain del Moro on the southern end, the material used to create the fountain is Portasanta; which is a rose marble.

In 1878, Antonio Della Bitta was asked to carve the statue of Nettuno slaying a giant octopus and Gregorio Zappala sculpted the group of 8 sea figures playing in the basin; two sea horses, two cherubs, two dolphins, and two sea nymphs. The fountain is as stunning as the others.

I took a long look over the lovely Piazza and walked to the café my friend and I had arranged to meet.

Taking a cappuccino at Piazza Navona will usually set you back a hefty 5 Euro (5.59 USD). For a small dinner you may have to pay a pricey 50 Euro (55.88 USD). However, having a cappuccino or even a glass of wine is worth it. It is lovely seeing the world go by on the beautiful square as you sit on one of Rome's most spectacular squares with amazing architecture. Street artists are always there to entertain the Piazza visitors; what else could you ask for?

Even Texel was enjoying her day out and was extremely well behaved. I was shocked and felt enormously proud at the same time. Many people stopped us to ask if they could pet her. She is very popular to the Italians as well as the tourists. Today, she has many requests to take a photo with her in front of a fountain or a monument. I think she knows she is a celebrity and is naturally photogenic. Most of the time she is a spoiled supermodel, but as I said before, she can be finicky; one day she is all "Oh, look at me" and posing well and the next she is a 'tom-boy' with no time to pose.

I spotted my friend, walked up to her, and hugged her. Texel seemed to feel slightly left out as she tried to come between us for her appropriate amount of attention. She's lucky she is an only child in our home.

We settled in at one of the many tables. In her usual fashion, Texel eyed the table next to us where everyone was eating sandwiches. Without warning, and not long after we arrived, she proceeded to bounce up onto the table and stole a sandwich. I was overcome with embarrassment. My dog clearly has no manners. The people at the next table appeared a little shocked too - to say the least. They were speechless as I hurried to gather my dog.

Many thoughts quickly ran through my mind. There I was all dolled up, ready to have a great day on the town, and my dog behaves like a little thief. Thankfully, these were tourists; tourists that found the incident rather amusing. They laughed at the situation light heartedly.

One of the waiters, however, did not find Texel amusing. He came out and told us we had to leave.

'Why?' I asked.

'Your dog is dirty,' he replied.

Without thinking, I blurted, 'You are dirty, your mother told me,' and walked away with Tex on leash.

My friend, running behind laughing, caught up to console me. I was upset, but to be truthful, my dog should never behave that way. She ruins our most treasured time together.

I should not have taken my anger out on the waiter because it is a fact that being a waiter in Italy is usually a job for life; there are no aspiring actors here. They take their job very seriously and expect respect from the people they serve.

Even though I knew I should not have barked at the waiter and I sometimes get very frustrated by people because of Texel, I am mostly frustrated with myself. I know I should be the one responsible for my dog, nobody else. I am responsible for her behavior. I try very hard to have her with me and sometimes that backfires. She doesn't mean harm.

Soon, when I thought everything was calm again and, although I was unjustifiably still angry with that waiter for calling Texel 'dirty,' I began breathing normally; that was until we walked slightly too close to Fontana del Moro. Texel suddenly and, without warning, jumped in.

For a moment, I thought we were Hollywood celebrities because I never had so many people take a photograph at one time; and all of my dog! Flashes everywhere!

I hurriedly dragged her out of the fountain and was lucky none of the Vigili (police) saw us.

My friend, still laughing, and I and Tex all walked to Largo di Torre Argentina - an area of ruins that borders Piazza Navona. This area is known as a 'cat sanctuary' and came about when the great Italian film star Anna Magnani (many may not know her; she was an actress born in 1908) was working at Teatro Argentina which borders the ruins.

Ms. Magnani spent her breaks feeding her four legged friends. This film legend, famous for her heart-tugging performances, died in the 1960's.

In 1993, others began helping feed, spay, and neuter the cats. The efforts soon became overwhelming and everyone realised there was more work than could be managed.

In one year, the cat population was ninety and growing due to the irresponsibility of people abandoning their cats and kittens; some went on vacation. And so, Torre Argentina Cat Sanctuary was born!

This was also a treat for Texel because she loves cats. I try to discourage her, but she always tries to play with them.

After all the commotion of the day, we walked into a good old-fashioned pub and had a beer and a sandwich. After a few sips of beer, I felt calm again and my initial reaction to start a fist-fight with the waiter had past. Thankfully. I hope he has forgotten us as well. My friend and I had a great day after all.

ONE LAST TIP: If you come to Rome at Christmas time and visit the Christmas market on Piazza Navona, please put on your warmest clothes. The wind is terribly cold on Piazza Navona. The two main entrances are opposite each other and this creates an intense flow of freezing air.

Chapter 13

BOOK BANTER

I was invited for lunch by my good friend Patrizia. She lives in Prati; a stylish and up market part of town bordering the Vatican State. Since she has a dog, she encouraged me to bring Texel.

So, away we went for another adventure. This would be Texel's first time on the Underground (a transportation system similar to the subway in New York City).

Termini is Rome's main train station, but it is also the central point for our two, yes two subway lines. The train station dates back to 1867. The original was demolished in 1937 to make space for a new station.

It is always hectic at the Termini, but if you have time to look around, the architecture is splendid. Riding the Underground was a good exercise for me and Tex because I am not permitted to take her on the escalator and I do not trust the elevators at Termini Station, so I took Texel in my arms and walked down the stairs.

Texel always makes me smile because she is so curious. I can take her anywhere and nothing fazes her. On the subway she is required to wear a muzzle, but even that never stops her from having fun.

Today, she sat with me on the subway and enjoyed the attention she always receives by others around her. She was utterly fascinated by the opening and closing of the train doors. One thing that did baffle her, though, was the voice she kept hearing announcing the next station. She could not figure out where that person was.

When we arrived at our destination, we exited the train and walked up the stairs. She trotted ahead of me; leading the way as though she was a well-experienced traveler and just so happened to travel the subway every day.

After a short walk, we came to Patrizia's apartment. She and I had a lovely time and the dogs rudely ignored each other.

This, however, made it even easier to enjoy Patrizia's beautiful garden; which, in Rome, is everyone's dream.

Patrizia's apartment is set back from a busy road. This provides privacy. Her living room has an enormous plush corner sofa that is easy to fall into and a little more difficult to get out of. Sometimes I think they made it to sleep on rather than sit on.

The artwork on her walls are from Italian painters. I don't know them, but they are stunning. The apartment is modern, but feels warm and inviting. The garden is off one side of her living room.

Most of the garden is paved and scattered all around are various luscious plants and palms. In a corner she has a rock formation fountain; which is ever so relaxing. She has an enormous parasol that can easily provide shade for six people. The sound of the water and the plants and cozy atmosphere of the garden make for a lovely afternoon.

As we enjoyed our time sitting sometimes and strolling sometimes in the garden, we discussed the crisis in Italy, gossiped, and drank exquisite cold white wine until it was time to walk the dogs. We felt the two of us managed to solve all the problems in the country and the world in general (ha ha).

After walking for a little while, Patrizia suggested we visit the Castel Sant'Angelo because below the castle is an ample grassy area that many people use to walk their dogs. We are permitted to let the dogs run off their leashes there.

The dogs played until the spring sun became too warm to enjoy any longer and, after all the wine, Patrizia and I quickly had enough as well.

After our great visit together, Patrizia and I said good-bye, hugged, and promised we would get together again soon. She walked back to her apartment as Tex and I walked to the Castel Sant'Angelo.

It's not a far walk and Texel was still filled with energy. I was happy just thinking about the lovely time we had with Patrizia and how we looked forward to more visits soon. It was always delightful to see her.

The Castel Sant'Angelo (Italian pronunciation: [kaˈstɛl sanˈtandʒelo]; English: Castle of the Holy Angel), is a towering cylindrical building in Rome.

It was initially commissioned by the Roman Emperor Hadrian as a mausoleum for himself and his family. The building was later used by the Popes as a fortress and castle, and is now a museum. The structure was once the tallest building in Rome.

Of all the monuments in Rome, Castel Sant'Angelo is my favorite and located on the Tiber River. Many times in the spring there is a market of some sort close to the Castel Sant'Angelo and the River. I was in luck today; there was a market alongside Castel Sant'Angelo.

I knew this would be a market after my own heart with lots of book stands and handmade clothes and jewelry; all of which are my favorite things.

I walked around the Castle and headed for the small market under the trees. As we walked and looked at the different stands in the cool shade of the lush trees, I felt a pang of happiness in my stomach when I stopped at a book stand.

Although I find reading in Italian still extremely difficult because they are written in 'passato remoto' - a past tense that does not exist in English - the smell of the old paper is like precious perfume to me.

I greeted the stand holder and picked up a random book. 'Salve,' I said.

'Salve' is only used in Rome and means 'hello.' It comes from the Latin verb 'salvēre' meaning 'being in good health.'

'Salve, signora,' he politely responded.

He jumped up from his seat and I received all of his attention. This is the treatment all tourists get; all smiles and compliments; but it only lasts until you give them your money.

Texel watched as I looked at various books. I can only imagine what she was thinking. I think her thoughts were something like '*this must be an invitation for me to do the same.*' So, she stood on her back paws and grabbed a book with her mouth.

Immediately, I scolded her, 'Give back that book, you horrible dog!' After quite the struggle, I managed to remove the book from her mouth. I was not successful at getting it out of her mouth quickly enough because the book was full of little teeth marks. Great! Now I was obligated to purchase the book.

The owner of the stand walked around and took the book from me. He said, 'Ma signora, non posso vendere un libro così!!!' (But madam, I can't sell a book like this)

'Lo so, mi dispiace tanto,' (I know, I am sorry) I replied.

'Anche a me dispiace, ma questo è il mio lavoro,' (I too am sorry, but this is how I make a living) he continued. While talking, he leaned slightly forward as though he was begging me to understand. A true actor!

'Allora, quanto costa?' (Okay, how much is it?) I asked.

'€15,' (16.81USD) he replied.

'Va bene,' (Okay) I agreed.

The way he carried on and made such a song and dance and fuss about Texel grabbing the book, it looked as if we were fighting to a group of German tourists standing nearby. We were not fighting; it is just the way things are done in Rome!

I paid for the book and, instead of it being an interesting biography or a memoir of a famous person, it turned out to be some boring engineering book.

After our huge fiasco at the bookstand, I took Texel and, on a short leash, we marched over the 'Angel Bridge' to take the bus back home.

The Aelian Bridge – known as Ponte Sant'Angelo - is an awesome Roman structure built between 133 and 134 AD to span the Tiber River and lead people into the Castel Sant'Angelo.

The bridge is faced with travertine marble and has five arches, three of which are Roman. The highlight of the structure, however, are the ten striking statues of angels inspired by the famous sculptor Gian L Bernini in 1667, by order of Pope Clement IX.

Rome is overflowing with beautiful art. On every corner, it seems, there's some gorgeous church or ancient fountain or stunning masterpiece from a famous artist for all visitors to see.

The Ponte Sant'Angelo, or Bridge of Angels, is one of these incredible sights. But unless you look closely, you'll miss its deeper meaning.

Bernini had a plan to perfectly fit the statues with the bridge's name and purpose. He wanted 10 statues, each holding something special relating to the suffering and crucifixion of Jesus. Bernini himself only finished the actual making of two Angels – the Angel with the Superscription "I.N.R.I" (Iesus Nazarenus Rex Iudaeorum (Jezus of Nazateth King of the Jews) and the Angel with the Crown of Thorns.

When Pope Clement IX saw how beautiful Bernini's two sculptures were, he decided the originals were too valuable to be placed outside and exposed to the elements. He had them replaced with copies and moved the sculptures into his private collection. They are now in the church Sant'Andrea delle Fratte. None the less, Bernini's design and vision of the bridge were kept in mind and were brought to life by his successors.

The statues are truly lovely.

Each sculptured angel symbolizes a part from the story of Jesus Christ's suffering and death by crucifixion. Gorgeous statues of the saints Peter and Paul watch over the entrance way of the bridge. The ten angels are:

The Angel with the Column
(Where Jesus was flogged)

The Angel with the Whips

The Angel with the Crown of Thorns

The Angel with Veronica's Veil

The Angel with His Garment and Dice
(Christ's garment that was gambled away)

The Angel with the Nails

The Angel with the Cross

144

The Angel with the Sponge

The Angel with the Lance

The Angel with the Superscription I.N.R.I.
Iesus Nazarenus Rex Iudaeorum
(Jezus of Nazateth King of the Jews.)
(The sign attached to the top of the Cross that said
"Jesus of Nazareth, King of the Jews")

After all the time with Patrizia, shopping, walking with

Texel, and admiring the beautiful Bridge of Angels, and more in

Rome, Tex and I rode the bus and finally made it home again.

Chapter 14

TEXEL TRAVELS

My husband and I had been working very hard for a while and felt in need of a well-deserved break. I dove into the computer and found an Agriturismo that allowed dogs.

An 'Agriturismo' is a farm that rents out rooms and small apartments; in short, a farm holiday.

We love these short breaks. The food comes straight from the land and the owners cook authentic Italian food. Also, nobody bothers you and we sleep like royalty; not a sound is heard other than the nocturnal animals; such as the owl and foxes and hares. For larger wildlife, one needs to be further inland. There you can find badgers, the door mouse, the stone marten and even bears in the province of Maremma. (Maremma is inland and is a province next to Lazio, which is part of Rome)

Texel loves these times away too.

I found an Agriturismo in Sabina. Sabina is a forty-minute drive east of Rome. Within these forty minutes you seem to travel into a time machine and, when you arrive, you are transported one hundred years back in time to a beautiful, lush, and silent place.

Here and there are the sounds of cows, horses, or sheep. The villages tend to be small with maybe three to four shops and a restaurant. It is so small that within one day everyone knows who you are and where you are staying. 'Our' Agriturismo was just outside one of these type villages.

We arrived mid-afternoon and parked the car. As we picked our luggage from the trunk, we heard steps behind us.

'Buonasera, Signor Alberto?' In Italy, in the afternoon or after lunch you say 'good evening' rather than 'good afternoon.' I still have problems with this. My mind still thinks of it as afternoon.

'Si,' my husband turned around and shook the woman's hand. I introduced myself and then proceeded to look around.

'Let me show you the apartment,' she said. We both nodded eagerly.

'Here it is 'Il Girasole,' (the sunflower) she said.

The Agriturismo was ideally situated on a hill with a fantastic view over the flowing hills.

It was a small one-bedroom apartment on the ground floor. Our host opened the window shutters and we were so happy! We had a breathtaking view of the Farfa Abbey.

We knew this would be a lovely view in the evening.

Farfa Abbey (Italian: *Abbazia di Farfa*) is a territorial abbey in northern Lazio, central Italy. It is one of the most famous abbeys of Europe. It belongs to the Benedictine Order and is located about 60 km from Rome.

An abbey is a type of church; however, there are only monks there and no nuns. They are self-sufficient, grow their own vegetables, and have livestock. The most famous monk who lived here was St. Francis.

As we gazed out the window, I eagerly imagined my husband and me and Tex sitting on our terrace, with a delicious glass of wine viewing the lovely abbey and other sites.

Then, the owner of the Agriturismo showed us where everything was in the little apartment. She also had a small map of the entire farm for us to explore. I heard her, but I never pay attention because I always leave those details of what is what and where to my husband. I like to explore things and was too busy taking in the panorama to listen closely enough.

'Will you be having dinner with us tonight?' I heard the owner ask.

'Yes, please. Is it okay if we bring our dog? She is well behaved.' (I felt my nose growing while speaking!!)

'That should be okay since we don't have many guests. The restaurant opens at 19:30,' she replied.

'Grazie a dopo,' (Thank you, we will see you later) my husband said as we looked at each other with happy faces.

Whenever we go somewhere, we always feel like two teenagers; young and in love.

Texel ran in circles trying to catch her tail; that's how excited she was to be at the Agriturismo. She must have understood she was invited to dinner; and we all know how she loves food.

Authentic Italian food is truly our favorite thing.

Some of the authentic Roman food you can enjoy in Italy is Cacio e Pepe. It sounds complicated but, in fact, it is very simple to prepare. All you need is pecorino (sheep cheese called Cacio in Roman slang), Romano cheese, and black pepper.

The only trick I find with this meal is that the proportions and the quality of the products determine its success or failure.

Using the best ingredients and measuring are important in making this dish. Cacio e Pepe is usually served with fresh long pasta such as spaghetti, linguine or tonnarelli.

Another authentic Italian meal is the delicious Bucatini all'Amatriciana. This is perhaps the world's most famous Roman dish as well as the subject of debates that can end the strongest of friendships and create insurmountable tensions on Christmas Eve – even more than global warming, civil unions, and veganism.

What should one use for Amatriciana? Guanciale (pork parts)? Or do you use garlic and onions or neither? Even in Italy, the Italians have many debates about which way is better. One great chef will say garlic while another claims it is better with onions. I know it's hard to believe, but an entire street fight can result from just discussing this. Italians are a bit 'mad' when it comes to their food!

Another amazing dish that is always very popular in Rome and even has fans among the ecclesiasts is spaghetti alla carbonara.

It is a very old dish that the carbonari (coal workers) - who had to watch over the burning coal for a long time - made directly over the coal fire from what they could carry in their pouches; items such as eggs, guanciale, pecorino and pasta.

Ask any Italian, it is literally to die for!!!Carbornara is always in a white sauce.

Carciofi alla Giudìa (Jewish-style Artichokes) is another of my favorites. It is Jewish-style artichokes that look like flowers. Those prepared at Nonna Betta, a kosher restaurant in Rome's Jewish ghetto, are extraordinary, as are the other dishes that blend Jewish traditions and Roman cuisine, such as the *tagliolini cacio e pepe* with chicory.

I am certain a brown and crispy bouquet of these fried artichokes can find their way into anyone's heart.

Food is on our 'to-do' list for later for sure. We thought it best to leave our luggage in the apartment and explore the surroundings rather than unpack our bags right away. There would be plenty of time for that after our meal.

On the website, the Agriturismo listed they had a small lake. Knowing how Texel loves to swim, we thought it would be nice to check this out first.

Texel had already found a pond when we arrived, but it was fenced. As we came closer, we understood why. There were ducks swimming in the pond!

We patted Texel's head and said, 'Sorry girl, but no swimming in there.' She kept running back and forth in front of the fence as we continued smiling at her; that was until we saw that she found a small hill and jumped over the enclosure!

My husband and I were instantly in a panic. First, we tried to get her back by shouting at her. When that did not work, we tried luring her to us with doggie treats (which we always carry for cases like these), and lastly we tried using sweet voices. Nothing worked. Texel had her mind made up; she wanted a duck!!

At this point, I could not help myself. I started laughing. My husband, who was not impressed, turned around and asked, 'What are you laughing at? This is serious. What if the owners see us!!!!?'

'I know,' I said, still laughing. 'Why don't you walk back to the Agriturismo and tell them we will have duck for dinner tonight.' Then my husband started laughing.

We were, however, no further along at getting Texel away from scaring those ducks. So, my husband, the brave one, jumped the fence and into the smelly duck pond he went to get Texel.

By this time, I was laughing so hard I had tears running down my cheeks. We all made it safely back to our apartment without being discovered. My husband marched straight into the shower with his clothes on. Afterwards, I soaked his clothes in water with my shampoo overnight.

Ducks are lovely, but their 'pooh' is disgusting for sure. To avoid another mishap, we kept Texel on her leash from then on. No more duck and dive episodes for her.

From that point on, we had an enjoyable stay at the Agriturismo and returned to Rome rested and well fed.

Chapter 15

ANXIOUS AT APPIA ANTICA

For a short time, my husband and I lived in a different area of Rome; in EUR with a beautiful top floor apartment with a stunning terrace. EUR is a residential and business district in Rome situated south of the city center. In this area there is a road called Appia Antica and a park with the same name. I know this can be confusing. Our apartment was nice, but never felt like home.

The area was chosen in the 1930s as the first site for the 1942 world's fair, which Benito Mussolini planned to open to celebrate twenty years of Fascism. The letters EUR standing for Esposizione Universale Roma (Universal Exposition Rome).

The project was originally called *E42* after the year in which the exhibition was planned to be held. EUR was designed to direct the expansion of the city towards the south-west and the sea and to be a new city center for Rome. Unfortunately, the planned exhibition never took place due to World War II.

There are a few nice areas in EUR but, unfortunately we did not live in those areas. We lived in an area still in Rome, just on the outskirts. The apartment we lived in belonged to my in-laws and they wanted us to live there. I remember we had a great view of some very ugly 1970's buildings as we looked out our front window.

Luckily, standing at the rear windows of the apartment, we had a view overlooking a wonderful park called the Appia Antica Park.

Our part of Appia Antica was intentionally kept wild so the wildlife could flourish. When I first discovered this park, I thought '*this will be fantastic for Texel.*' Although I did not like the area in which we now lived, I felt the park and the apartment were enough to leave my beloved San Lorenzo.

The first time Texel and I walked in the park, however, I realized how careful we needed to be. First, when others said the park was kept *wild*, they meant it!! We followed one path that suddenly stopped. Another path took us to another abrupt end of the sidewalk. Here, we stood at the top of a deep ravine looking down into a pit! This made for a 'not so relaxing' of a walk!

In addition to all the 'ends' of pathways, the park was filled with foxtails. Foxtails are that horrible grass that looks a bit like wheat, but can work their way into a dog's ear, nose or the skin between the toes to make their way into the body of the animal. Each time we finished our walks, I spent at least a half hour removing foxtails from my precious girl.

On the other side of the park where the beautiful Via Appia Antica runs; which is where my in-laws lived. I need to mention again that Appia Antica is both a park and a road.

Appia Antica road – where my in-laws live - is one of

the most important roads in Rome because it connects Rome to Brindisi in the southeast area of Italy.

Appia Antica road reminds us that Rome is in the center of everything and all the roads begin at Rome and radiate out from the city. This is how the saying, "All roads lead to Rome" was born. All roads literally do lead to Rome in Italy.

"All roads lead to Rome" appears in the Latin form *mīlle viae dūcunt hominēs per saecula Rōmam* meaning "a thousand roads lead men forever to Rome"

Now, back to my side of Appia Antica. I tried to enjoy the local dog park with Texel, but was not impressed by the people or their dogs. I thought it was a very unfriendly park; not at all like the others I have loved in Rome.

Also, I came from San Lorenzo where I always met somebody on the street for a chat. Now, in this new apartment, my life was very lonely.

So, with Tex as my only friend, we returned to the wild field of the Appia Antica Park behind our house and made sure to always walk the same route. We knew if we took another path, it may lead to a dead end or we may find ourselves standing on the edge of another ravine. I was not going to put the life of Tex or myself in danger.

One day, while on our usual walk, I tripped over a stone. I went down like a ton of bricks and WOW! did it hurt! I used my hands to lessen the fall and this resulted in the palms of my hands being skinned and bleeding.

I began nursing my sore bottom with my bloody hands and, by the time I managed to get back on my feet, Texel had left me and continued walking. I assumed she continued walking our usual route, but when I arrived at the end of the walkway, she was not there.

My heart stopped for a second as I asked myself, '*Where is Texel?*' I forgot all about my sore bum and hands.

I frantically ran up and down the paths on our route shouting, '*Texel, Texel, where are you?*' I ran our course four times. I looked in all the places where she could have gone - including the possibility of falling down into the ravine - but could not find her anywhere.

By this time, unable to find her, I was crying. I could not believe I lost her. Was she in pain? Had someone taken her? The craziest scenarios went through my mind. Would I ever see my precious dog again?

All of the sudden, my cell rang. I answered with a broken voice.

"P-Pronto?" I asked. (Pronto, is how the telephone is answered in Italy, a bit like an American 'Hello?' Pronto has more pressing meaning, it also means 'I am ready!')

"Do you own a Golden Retriever named Texel?" the caller asked.

"Yes, I do. Where is she?" I asked.

"She is in front of the bar on the square," the caller continued.

"Arrivo," (I am on my way) I said and started running towards the bar.

When I arrived in front of the bar, Texel was laying on the pavement in the sun as though nothing had transpired; as though she was never lost. I jumped on her and cuddled her until she could not stand it any longer.

The people in the bar came out to see the spectacle. Nothing much happens in EUR, so if you see a crazy foreigner hugging and crying over her dog, covered in blood, you go and have a look. I am sure our episode was the subject of conversation at the dinner table for many weeks on the square where we lived.

"You are lucky we called you," the bar owner said.

"I sure am. Thank you so much, grazie mille," I said with all the sincerity in my heart.

I was so upset at the thought of losing Texel, but now was relieved. I asked the owner to pour me a glass of wine. I felt I deserved this after almost losing my best girl.

Tex and I never went back to the field behind our home after my almost losing her. My husband and I moved back into our little apartment in San Lorenzo that does not even have a small balcony – but this to us is home! And there is no place like home in Rome for me, my husband, and Texel.

EPILOGUE

I sincerely hope you have enjoyed a few of the many adventures of Texel and me. I apologize to all the people in this book who are terrified of dogs.

San Lorenzo, where I live, is a very dog-friendly place and I sometimes make the mistake that all other areas offer the same hospitality.

If you are ever in Rome, I suggest you visit San Lorenzo. It is an evening spot. We have very few shops, but all the more pubs, bars and restaurants.

Sapienza University keeps the area feeling young. Sapienza is a village in itself. It houses 130 thousand students made up of young adults who believe they can change the world. They are idealistic and optimistic. I love them for that!!!

Another interesting site most people do not know about is cemetery Verano; also in San Lorenzo. The last King Pope, Pio IX, died in 1878. After him, Popes do not have the title "King" any longer. He is not laid to rest in the Vatican, but the Basilica in San Lorenzo. His body is displayed in a glass coffin and most find it a very peaceful and spiritual sight. The Basilica also contains a shrine of St. Lawrence, Pope St. Cyprian & St Stephen.

The Verano is well worth a visit because it's off the main tourist trail and you can enjoy a look around because the relaxed nature of the area allows the time and space to take a look around.

Other various celebrities, Alberto Sordi, (actor) Roberto Rossellini (Director), Vittorio de Sica (Actor), Vittorio Gassman (Actor), Marcello Mastroianni (Actor), and Carlo Pedersoli AKA Bud Spencer (Actor) are buried there. Guided tours are available.

It is a stunning cemetery that also hosts the Jewish Cemetery. Rome does not have an Eruv.

Although I will never be an Italian, I am proud to call myself a San Lorenzina.

I hope you have enjoyed my little book of Havoc in Rome.

About the Author

I am Ingrid. I am originally from the Netherlands. I have traveled the world, but mostly I have made my home in London. London is where I met my husband, Alberto, who took me to Rome, Italy where we have been living for the past 15 years.

My biggest buddy in Rome is Texel or, as I at times, affectionately call her, Tess. After the loss of our previous

Golden, Neve, (which means "Snow" in Italian) I felt something missing in our lives. We went to the beach, but did not enjoy it. We took a vacation, but got bored after only one short week.

My social life in Rome was down to zero before I found Texel.

Although my husband was not yet ready, I heard through a friend that her neighbor had a litter of Golden puppies. I persuaded my husband to go and have a look. So we took the car and drove into the countryside east of Rome, where a lady breeds wonderful and lovely Golden Retrievers and Newfoundlanders.

Well, as everyone knows, whoever goes to have a look at a litter of these little fluffs and does not fall in love, must have a gene (or two) missing. I picked out the one that came running to me. Her name is Texel.

Texel is actually an Island in the Netherlands, which is pronounced, 'Tessel.' In the very beginning, I knew my husband felt he was betraying our previous Golden, Neve, who passed away several years before, but now Texel and my husband are the biggest friends. An added bonus is that my social connections are back to normal. Texel is a people magnet. (At least a 'dog people' one.)

Along with my dog, Texel, and all our adventures in Rome, I work as a Life Purpose Coach and teach English as a foreign language.

I wrote this little book to share some of the happy memories I am making with Texel and share the beauty of our homeland, Rome.

ACKNOWLEDGEMENTS

I would like to take the time to thank:

Lee Sizemore, my editor and publisher at A 2 Z Press LLC for her creative mind and helpful manner. Her experience, patience and professionalism has taught me so much. Lee is a pleasure to work with.

I want to thank my wonderful friend, Marjan Rahimi, for her lovely illustrations. She always makes me happy as she captures the moments of havoc for Texel and me in Rome.

I want to thank Isabella Ruggieri for her gracious gift of our cover photo.

Abbraci (hugs), Ingrid.

CPSIA information can be obtained
at www.ICGtesting.com
Printed in the USA
LVHW050828010819
626079LV00005B/31/P